The Retford War Memorial

Heroes of World War I

Ken Hoddy   Tim Bethell

Editors Paul & Angela Meads

First published 2014
Bookworm of Retford
1 Spa Lane, Retford Notts, DN22 6EA
www.bookwormretford.co.uk

A catalogue record of this book is available from the British Library
The Retford War Memorial, Heroes of World War I
ISBN 9780992785710

Printed and bound by Burgess Design and Print, Beehive Street, Retford.
www.burgessdesignandprint.com

Contents

I would like to express my gratitude to the following: The Town Council and the Mayors and Councillors who have always been there to help in any way, such as the care given to the garden of remembrance by the Town's Parks Department; also The Fellowship of the Services, 272 Retford Cannon Mess, who provided the two planters for wooden crosses; all the Retfordians who subscribed to the building of the memorial and again to its restoration fund; Wendy Quigley for her support when the memorial was vandalised, and Jim Napier, Graham Oxby, Ian Campbell and Alan Chambers. And finally, thanks go to Mick Bradford and to Retford Memorials, who have restored and maintained the memorial to a high standard.

Our wonderful Memorial holds "names, just names", but when you look more closely you will find names listed several times as the war took brothers, fathers and sons from the same families. Families with multiple losses include the Davison family with six losses, and the Breddy, Dixon, Ostick, Taylor and Patterson families, who all had four losses. What pain the families had to endure knowing their loved ones had died in a far-off land! We hope this book tells the story of these heroes: men and women who are the pride of our town. They had valuable lives in Retford before having to serve their country, never to return... so we could be free.

Looking to the future, I see that there will always be a need for a fund to enable our war memorial to be maintained and repaired, and so it has been arranged for the profit from the sale of this book to go into the 'Retford War Memorial Restoration Fund'. Donations can also be made directly to the fund's account held at The National Westminster Bank, Market Square, Retford, DN22 8DL

Ken Hoddy 2014
(Memorial Custodian and Fund Co-ordinator)

The Retford War Memorial

After the Armistice had been signed on 11th November 1918 there began a great outpouring of emotion. The Great War had never seen soldiers, nurses and civilians killed on such a scale before. People started to go on pilgrimages to see the graves of their relatives and to try to make sense of their losses, but this often favoured the rich. It was realised that the majority of people at home were unable to make these trips, but required places where they could go and pay their respects, and have a permanent memorial of their loved ones. Up and down the country committees were formed and discussions began to look at the ways in which those people who had died in the War would always be remembered.

The Retford memorial was paid for by public subscription and designed by architect Leonard W Barnard F.R.I.B.A. of Cheltenham. The memorial was constructed of Sandcliffe Stone from Darley Dale, Derbyshire, and the contractors were R. L Boulton and Sons of Cheltenham. The final cost was £1,806-10s-0d. Our Memorial is in the shape of an Eleanor Cross, an octagonal structure of the late Gothic style and rises to some 23 feet above ground level. On the eight panels are the names of 306 men killed in the 1914-1918 war.

In 1951, bronze plaques were added to the Memorial, giving the names of the 110 soldiers who died in the 1939-1945 war. These plaques were unveiled and dedicated on 6th May 1951. The entire cost was met by the Retford and District National Savings Committee.

In 2007 it was noticed that the Memorial was in a poor state of repair and so the Memorial Restoration Committee was formed, which consisted of a group of dedicated individuals who worked hard over two years to raise the £20,000 required to meet the costs of its restoration. To restore our Memorial to its former glory, the work was carried out by a local firm, Retford Memorials. The rededication service took place on Sunday 17th August 2008.

Retford 1914

In 1914 the people of Retford would have been busying themselves around this small market town, following their normal daily routines. The majority of the Retford people would have had some knowledge of the growing crisis in Europe: local papers like the Retford Times, and weekly pictorial newspapers for the masses were very common by the early twentieth century and, thanks to twenty or so years of compulsory and free (if rudimentary) education, the majority could read.

Undoubtedly, the possibility of the outbreak of war and the growing crisis in Europe would have been put to the back of Retfordian's minds, as the day before the assassination of Archduke Franz Ferdinand and his wife in Sarajevo (28th June 1914), Retford was visited by King George V and Queen Mary. The calamitous event in Sarajevo became the catalyst for hostilities in future months and years, the like of which nobody could have foreseen. These took place not only in Europe, but worldwide. Immediately following the assassination, political wheels were whirring and ententes and agreements were invoked. Ultimately Britain was brought into the conflict because of a little-known treaty (the Treaty of London) signed in 1839, which guaranteed Belgium's independence and neutrality. As part of their war plan (Schlieffen Plan*), Germany invaded Belgium in August 1914. As Germany were now in violation of the Treaty of London, the British declared war on Germany on 4th August 1914.

The new education system did so much to instil an enormous sense of pride and devotion to the King and Empire that when the call for volunteers was made in August and September 1914 men joined up in droves. Thanks to the newspapers (as already described), working men were well aware that the British Empire had made a promise to Belgium and the patriotic fervour ensured a plentiful supply of volunteers ready and willing to help.

Being aware of the crisis and the ensuing declaration of war, the Territorial Army based in Retford were soon in action. On Saturday 7th August 1914 the National Reserve (effectively the Territorial Army) presented itself to HQ on Exchange Street. At this meeting it was agreed that two route marches a week should take place, to help with physical fitness. The first route march took place the following Monday, 10th August 1914. Fifty men fell in outside the Swan on Carolgate. The men marched up Albert Road, Cobwell Road to Babworth School House and then to the Great North Road via Lady Bridge Road before returning home.

At this time, early August, the local Territorial Army had 93 men who reported for duty: 23 signed up to Class 1 duties, i.e. willing to serve abroad; 49 signed up for home service only, i.e. Class 2; and 21 signed up for local service only, i.e. Class 3.

The local Yeomanry Regiment, the Sherwood Rangers, departed for Diss on Tuesday 10th August at 8.30 p.m. following a service held on the previous Sunday in East Retford Church. Prior to their departure, billets for the men had been found in the Corn

Exchange, Messrs Denman's Hall, the Conservative Club, the Wesleyan School and various inns in the town.

The Sherwood Rangers Squadrons being deployed were from Worksop, Mansfield, Newark and Retford.

In September 1914 an advert was placed in the Retford Times asking for recruits to bring the regiment up to full strength as they had volunteered for Foreign Service. This was the forerunner to Kitchener's famous poster Your Country Needs You, first published in The Times on 5th September 1914.

Between 4th September and 17 August 1914 the Retford Office had recruited 166 recruits: 127 for General Service, 6 for Special Reserve and 38 for Cavalry, Artillery and regiments other than County regiments.

Heroes on the Memorial
from World War I

1914

CAPTAIN CYRIL OSWALD DENMAN-JUBB
2nd Battalion Duke of Wellington's (West Riding Regiment).
Killed 24th August 1914.

Though he lived in Ireland, Cyril was born in Retford in 1876. His previous military career had included service in South Africa between 1899 and 1902.

He was killed in the first big battle involving British troops in the war, the Battle of Mons. His regiment was involved in a rearguard action and sustained many casualties.

Cyril Denman-Jubb is buried in Hautrage Military Cemetery, Belgium.

RIFLEMAN GEORGE LIVERSIDGE
2680 2nd Battalion King's Royal Rifle Corps.
Died 14th September 1914.

In an edition of the Retford Times in August 1915 the death of Rifleman George Liversidge was finally confirmed by the War Office. George had been a regular soldier with the King's Royal Rifles through the Boer War, as well as serving in Malta and Egypt. Although stated as missing after the Battle of the Aisne, confirmation of his death was almost a year later. At that time in 1914 a fellow soldier of George's had written to the family saying he had been killed, having been shot through the head. A further letter was received at the same time from Captain Bury of the same regiment stating that Rifleman George Liversidge went out with seven or eight more soldiers to reconnoitre positions in front. None of them returned and their bodies were never found.

Having spent nine years with the forces, George left in 1909 and took up employment at Messrs. Jenkins as a furnace man. Throughout this period George lived with his parents, Amos and Mary Liversidge, on Whitehall Road, Retford. George was thirty-two years of age at the time of his death. Having no known grave, George Liversidge's name lives on La Ferte-sous-Jouarre Memorial in France, along with two other Retfordians, John Bacon Robinson and Bertie Townrow.

PRIVATE JOHN BACON ROBINSON
4795 2nd Coldstream Guards.
Died 15th September 1914.

'Retford Soldier Killed': Retford Times 9th October 1914
The death of Pte John Bacon Robinson of the 2nd Coldstream Guards was reported in the Retford Times of 9th October, although he had been killed on 15th September 1914. He was the son of John Robinson, 3 Thrumpton Lane, Retford, who at one stage kept the Durham Ox. Pte Robinson was thirty-four when he died.

John was an accomplished violinist and was educated at the Wesleyan School. Pte Robinson would have terminated his time as a reservist three days after he was called up. John had arranged to be married when, sadly, he had to rejoin his regiment. The Robinson family had another son, Arthur, serving at the Front with the Royal Engineers. John's name appears on La Ferte-sous-Jouarre Memorial carrying the names of 3740 soldiers of the BEF who died in August, September and the early part of October during the Battle of the Aisne.

PRIVATE CAMPBELL CAWARD (CAYWOOD, CAWOOD)
7634 2nd Battalion King's Own Borderers
Killed 13th October 1914.

PRIVATE JOHN MICHAEL MARSH
7633 2nd Battalion King's Own Borderers
Died 14th October 1914.

Private John Marsh

Whilst researching Campbell's details I have come across three different ways of spelling his surname: Caywood in the Retford Times, Cawood on the Retford War Memorial. The spelling provided from the CWGC and the SNWM, Caward, is believed to be the correct one.

It would appear that Campbell Caward Snr was born in Retford in 1843. Campbell Snr appears in the 1871 census as a twenty-five-year-old living as a lodger in the house of Frederick Stadward, 10 Booths Yard, Doncaster. At this time he was employed as a slater.

1881 finds Campbell Snr back in Retford living at 15 St John Street. Campbell Snr, now thirty-five, is shown to be married to Elizabeth, (thirty-two, born in Birkenhead) and having a one-year-old daughter, Susan, who was born in Sheffield. The census shows Campbell Snr still to be employed as a slater.

By 1891 the family was living at Woolpack Street, Retford. By this time Campbell Snr had been widowed and Campbell Jnr, six years old, had appeared. By 1901 Campbell Snr, aged fifty-six, was living on his own in Beck Row, North Retford. The name by now was being spelt Caywood.

Campbell Caywood Jnr, as a reservist, rejoined his regiment on 4th August 1914, having enlisted in the army thirteen years previously and having seen service in Egypt, India, Ireland and Africa. Campbell won a marksmanship competition in Cairo in which there were 1,300 other competitors. Pte Caywood's father had also seen service and, as reported in the Retford Times, "had in his possession an old horse pistol which he picked up on the battlefield of Khartoum".

On 11th September 1914 a rumour was circulating around Retford that Pte Campbell Caywood of the KOSB (Cawood on the memorial) had met his death.

The Retford Times of 18th September reported: "Very little news of Pte Campbell Caywood of the KOSB has been received by his relatives in Retford. Pte Breddy of Spital Hill, home on leave, stated that he had seen him once on the Continent.

Under the headline 'A Sad Coincidence: Two Retford Men Killed' The Retford Times reported that 'two more men have to be added to the Retford Roll of Honour' when the deaths of Pte John Marsh and Campbell Cayward of the King's Own Scottish Borderers were reported as killed in action. The report continued that these 'two brave men had been friends all their life and it is sad that they should die together on the battlefields fighting for their country's honour.'

Both men as lads went to St Saviour's School and they enlisted together 13 years ago, their numbers being 7733 and 7734. Both had served in Egypt, India, Ireland and South Africa."

On 12th October the KOSB were ordered to attack Cuinchy. The attack did not last long, with 'D' Company meeting heavy fire in which their commander Major William Lynn Allen was killed and ten others were killed, wounded or missing. 'A' Company, although heavily opposed, were able to consolidate the ground they had won.

According to Ray Westlake's 'British Battalions in France & Belgium 1914'
12th - took part in attack on Cuinchy
13th - engaged around Annequin
14th - no mention (typical!)
15th - relieved and to Beuvry

Extract from 'The K.O.S.B. in The Great War' by Capt. Stair Gillon (pp48-9):

'On 12th the bad news came that the French had lost Vermelles, 2 miles S. of Annequin. The language problem had already started, when the K.O.S.B. were relieved by the arrival of other battalions of the 13th I.B., and were ordered forthwith, i.e. at 4 pm, to attack Cuinchy between the road (S.) and the canal (N.) towards La Bassee. Beyond the canal were the Dorsets [1st Bn.] slightly in advance of the K.O.S.B.; on their R. were the D. of W. [2nd Duke of Wellington's (West Riding)]. The attack did not last long.

'D' on the L. met with heavy fire, which killed Major Allan (from whom Captain Caird took over) and 2nd Lieut. Woollcombe, a true son of the regiment. Dalrymple was wounded, and there were 10 other casualties. 'A' were also opposed strongly, but the C.O. was able to reinforce before 5 pm and, before 6 pm, to intimate consolidation of the ground then won...'

Next day it was hoped with the aid of a field-gun to press forward, and a start ordered for 5.30, as part of a larger operation in which the 3rd Division were taking part. The K.O.S.B. still pointed towards Cuinchy and the D. of W. faced Auchy. It was for a brilliant bit of patrol-leading that Sgt. J. Skinner won his first honour in the Great War - the D.C.M. A/C.S.M. H. Pike was similarly honoured.

On 13th, once more the Dorsets N. of the canal were ahead, and by 10 a.m. had halted E. of Givenchy and offered help by oblique fire. But an advance of a furlong was the utmost the K.O.S.B. could achieve, and it was reported that the D. of W. were similarly consolidating. So there they also consolidated. As is well known, the Dorsets came in for a terrible shelling: 13 officers were killed and more than half the battalion were killed, wounded, or missing. They were withdrawn to Pont Fixe. Our battalion had 60 casualties (k. and w.), besides losing 2nd Lieut. MacRae, who died on 14th, and Capt. Smith, who could ill be spared, and Caird, both wounded. The 13th was therefore another sombre day for the Borderers. On 14th Coke [Major - C.O.] was in suspense all day. No messenger could pass from Connell [Capt. - O.C. firing line], and it was only realized, after relief by the 256th Inf. Regt. of the French, that the K.O.S.B. had smothered what might have developed into an attack en masse, by steadiness and good musketry. 2nd Lieut. H.J. Harvey was wounded. The French took over speedily and silently about 2 a.m. on the 15th, and the K.O.S.B. marched back in the small hours 2 miles to Beuvry utterly exhausted."

It is likely that both Campbell and John were killed in action at the Battle of La Bassee, and they are remembered on the Le Touret Memorial in the Pas de Calais, France.

PRIVATE BERTIE WILLIAM TOWNROW
9988 1st Battalion West Yorkshire (Prince of Wales Own)
Killed 20th September 1914.

The town of Retford was thrown into mourning again on 30th October 1914 when another Retfordian, Pte Townrow, aged twenty, son of Mrs Townrow of Bolton Lancs, was reported as having been killed. Mrs Townrow received the following intimation from the War Office: "It is my duty to inform you that a report has this day been received from the War Office notifying the death of Pte Townrow of the 1st West Yorkshire Regiment, and I am to express to you the sympathy and regret of the Army Council at your loss. The cause of death was killed in action". Pte Townrow had actually been killed on 20th September 1914.

Pte Townrow was in the Sherwood Rangers Yeomanry for two years before enlisting in the regular army in 1912/1913. Another son of Mrs Townrow, Walter, who enlisted in Sheffield at the commencement of the war, was based with the 3rd Battalion West Yorkshire Regiment. Records show that Walter survived the war.

It is likely that Pte Townrow was killed during the action on the Aisne Heights. The Northern Banks of the River Aisne form a continuous slope up to the Chemin des Dames, an ancient road. This position formed an excellent defensive position for the retreating German Army. The Allies were given orders to capture crossings and to continue their attack up the steep slope that formed the northern banks of the Aisne. The 18th Brigade, of which the 1st West Yorkshires were part, crossed the river at Bourg. Over the next three days, 18th-20th September, attempts were made to reach the top and secure a hold on the Chemin des Dames. The Germans, however, had such a commanding view of the area that they were able to dominate the situation. The fighting was often bitter and hand-to-hand and took place on difficult and often wooded terrain. The Germans were able to entrench themselves and the failure of the British Army to break through when the Germans were in disarray undoubtedly prolonged the war as the race for the Channel began.

His name is commemorated on La Ferte-sous-Jouarre Memorial.

ABLE SEAMAN VALENTINE WILLIAM ROGERS 200458 and
1st Class Stoker **GEORGE WILLIAM GAUTREY** 300802
Both drowned on the HMS Good Hope at the Battle of Coronel 1st November 1914

On Friday 27th November the headline in the Retford Times read:
'On The Good Hope - Victims from Retford and District'
There were several men belonging to Retford and District who were on the HMS Good Hope when it foundered during action with a German Squadron off the Chilean coast. In the Official List published last Monday (23rd November) of officers and men missing after the disaster appear the names mentioned below. 'In the absence of evidence to the contrary it is feared', says an Admiralty Communication, 'that those enumerated in the list have lost their lives in the engagement,'

One of the men to perish was Able Seaman Valentine William Rogers, thirty-two, who was postman for Eaton, Gamston, Rockley and West Drayton. Very sadly, Rogers's wife had died on 11 May 1914 and he had been left with a baby of two weeks. His sister in Nottingham, however, took the baby. He was in the Reserve and had been called up for the usual month's training in July 1914, never to return. Rogers was to die in the fateful action on 1st November 1914, off the coast of Chile, which was to become known as the Battle of Coronel.

Another local man to die in the Battle of Coronel was George William Gawtrey (Gautrey), aged thirty-four, son of Mr and Mrs Gawtrey, who lived at George Inn Yard, Retford. George, who was a 1st Class Stoker, left a widow and two daughters, who at the time of his death were living at 25 Howard Road, Mansfield. Like Valentine Rogers, George Gawtrey was called up in July, never to return home. Before the outbreak of the war he was employed at Langwith pit. The Retford Times reported that the sad news was distressing as Mrs Gawtrey was seriously ill, and that two of her brothers were also serving, George Keyworth with HMS Antrim and William Keyworth who is with the Notts and Derby Regiment.

Thirty-year-old Able Seaman Herbert Bull, who also met his death on that fateful day, originally lived on Wharton Street, Retford and attended the National School. The family moved to Grimsby in 1902. He joined the Navy in 1909.

Other local men who died were Able Seaman Horace William Varley, who lived in Gainsborough and William Shipley of Sutton-on- Trent, also a 1st Class Stoker.

HMS Good Hope, Flagship of Admiral Cradock, sunk on 1st November 1914 along with HMS Monmouth. There were no survivors from either cruiser - a total of nearly 1600 men died.

PRIVATE WILLIAM TAYLOR
5907 1st Battalion Lincolnshire Regiment (9th Brigade).
Died 1st November 1914.

In the Retford Times of 18th December 1914, under the headline 'Retford Man Killed in Action', the death was announced of William Taylor, a private in the 1st Lincolns. Pte Taylor actually died on 1st November 1914. Employed as a bricklayer's labourer before the outbreak of hostilities, William Taylor, a reservist, was recalled to his regiment on August Bank Holiday 1914. Taylor, well known in Retford, resided at 41 St John's Street, and on his death sadly left a widow and two children.

The Retford Times reported that the last time Mrs Taylor had heard from William was a letter on 20th October 1914. In this letter the soldier said that he was "getting on alright" and that the Lincolns had been christened the "Gun Pinchers".

'The Captured Guns by the Lincolns' (Retford Times, 27th Nov 1914)
'Private W Smith [Egmanton, Tuxford] of the 1st Lincs took part in the Battle of Soissons, where the Lincolns, despite heavy shrapnel fire, captured seven guns. The Colonel asked permission of the General to try to get to the guns. He led the men through a wood with only his map as a guide. He took 'C' and 'D' companies with him, leaving 'A' and 'B' in support. They crept through and took up a position outside, quite unobserved by the enemy. The order to fix bayonets was given and the Commander, Colonel Smith, gave the order to charge, and the Germans were slaughtered by their guns. As soon as they saw them they started to run. The Lincolns, however, got home with the bayonet on those within reach, and the Royal Scots came up and mounted guard until the Artillery fetched them away. All the guns were in working order. The men of the Lincolns received congratulations from General French and General Shaw. The Lincolns were the first regiment to fire a shot in France and the first to capture any guns.'

The report went on to print an extract of a letter sent in December 1914 to Mrs Skelton of the Red Lion, Carolgate, from William Taylor's brother, Lance Corporal Taylor (6 West Street), also of the 1st Lincolns. The letter acknowledges the fact that he had received some "smokes sent to him by friends" and that "he would like to spend Christmas in Retford." In the letter he mentions the death of his brother but gives no details.

Sadly, the family were to suffer another loss later in the war when Thomas Taylor, another brother, was to die whilst serving with the Sherwood Foresters.

Pte William Taylor died during the second month of the first battle Of Ypres. A long artillery barrage on the trenches between Wytschaete and Messines started at dusk on 31st October 1914, and ended at midnight. One hour later, nine battalions of the

6th Bavarian Guard attacked the village of Wytschaete. A Composite Cavalry group of just 415 men defended the village. There followed several counter-attacks and attacks by the Composite Cavalry and the enemy. Finally they were unable to maintain their position and withdrew to the west of the village. Two battalions from II Corps (1st Lincolnshires and the 1st Northumberland Fusiliers) were sent up to support what was left of the cavalry and orders were given to retake the village. They came under intense rifle fire, artillery and enfilading machine guns and had to break off the attack. The result was a loss of 301 Lincolnshires and 98 Northumberland Fusiliers. William Taylor was one of the men lost.

William Taylor has no known grave and is commemorated on the Menin Gate in Ypres, Belgium.

PRIVATE CHARLES LEVICK
9141 1st Battalion Northumberland Fusiliers
Killed 12 November 1914.

The first soldier to be reported as having been killed in 1915 was Pte Charles Levick, 1st Battalion Northumberland Fusiliers. He was actually killed on 12th November 1914. It is likely that Pte Levick died in the final stages of the 1st Battle of Ypres at an area in and around Nonne Boschen Wood.

Fighting alongside other regular soldier battalions such as the 1st Lincolns, the 1st Royal Scots and the 4th Royal Fusiliers, they subdued attack after attack by German Forces.

The odds were 5:1 in favour of the Germans, but by rapid rifle fire and shelling they kept the Germans at bay, but not with heavy losses.

Eventually the Prussian Guard who were involved in the attack retreated after sustaining heavier losses than the British and this more or less ended the 1st Battle of Ypres and the parts around Nonne Boschen where Charles Levick lost his life.

Pte Levick, a native of Retford, was the third son of Mr and Mrs J C Levick of 12 New Street. Charles attended the National School in Retford under the close tutelage of Mr T Daffen.

Charles served his time as a soldier with the "Fighting Fifth", so-called as they were the Fifth Regiment of Foot before becoming the Northumberland Fusiliers, and possibly due to a remark made by Wellington during the Peninsula War: "The ever-fighting, often tried, but never-failing Fifth." Soon after enlisting he was sent to South Africa and later to India. Pte Levick saw action in the South African War, at the Battle of Belmont, as well as many other encounters with the enemy; he also gained a medal for services in the North West Frontier.

On leaving the army, having returned from India in 1911, Charles secured employment as a postman in Newark, being transferred to Worksop where he was employed for nine months before being called up for active service in the first week of 1914. Sadly, his period as a reservist was due to end in January 1915.

Pte Levick has no known grave and is commemorated on the Menin Gate, Ypres, Belgium.

PRIVATE GEORGE JOHN TOMLINSON
6855 1st Battalion Lincolnshire Regiment.
Killed 4th November 1914.

'Mr John Tomlinson of 57 Spital Hill, Retford, had two sons in the army: Pte George John Tomlinson, 1st Lincolnshire's, formerly postman at Maltby, and Pte Leonard Tomlinson, Yorks and Lancs. A letter received from George was partially printed in the Retford Times read:

"Just a few lines hoping you are in the best of health. I am in the pink of condition. You will no doubt think I am a long time writing this, but you must know we cannot write just when we like. I am getting about tired of it, but hope to get through the lot of it, as you know this is what we call real war. In fact I am just getting used to it. We are mostly under fire. You don't see many sad faces with all our troubles. The men make light of it singing and laughing as if nothing was happening. You would be surprised what a difference there has been lately. I will tell you one day if I live to come back and I do hope so. I think I have seen a little since we started at Mons and Cambrai, and the capture of the guns, which you no doubt will have read of in the papers. We had a nasty go just after that. We had to shift them with a toothpick at the end of the gun. Talk about them running, hockey was not in it. I am pleased to think I have more brothers who are doing their duty. I wish them luck as I think I have been very lucky up to now. My best regards to all enquiring friends.'

'Retford Soldier Killed': Retford Times, December 25th 1914
'Mr and Mrs J Tomlinson, 57 Spital Hill, Retford, received the sad news on Saturday that their eldest son, Private Geo Tomlinson, 1st Lincolnshire Regiment was killed in actionon 14 November 1914 at a place not stated. A leaflet was enclosed signed by Lord Kitchener intimating that "The King commands me to assure you of the true sympathy of His Majesty and the Queen in your sorrow".

Pte. Tomlinson was a reservist and when recalled to the colours in August 1914 he only had a few months to complete his service. He was a postman at Maltby and leaves a widow. Writing his last letter home, dated November 5th, the deceased soldier said,

"I am just enjoying a few days at ease and I can do with it. I am not very well. I think it is only a cold. I could do with a 'bust up' just for a change. I don't worry, much as it is no good. There are lots of things I would like, but I think I can manage until Christmas, when from what I read in the papers we are to receive presents. We have cold nights. We have plenty of clothes, but it is the wet that is the worst. We have some nice weather at times, but I don't think I shall bother for a holiday out here. I think I am a cat of nine lives. The men who came out with us have nearly all gone. I am only just alive as we have had it a bit rough. I am lucky to get out of it, but here I am - a slight tap. It is a fight, but we must expect it. I don't think the people of England seem to realise what it is like out here. Grande and Taylor went under yesterday with about 500. We had altogether a loss of 1200."

Mr and Mrs Tomlinson have another son, Leonard, in the York and Lancaster Regiment now serving at the front.'

George Thompson is commemorated on the Menin Gate at Ypres, Belgium.

PRIVATE WILLIAM JAMES WADE
2026 Nottinghamshire Yeomanry (Sherwood Rangers).
Died 19th December 1914.

Private William James Wade was forty-one when he died serving with the Nottinghamshire Yeomanry (Sherwood Rangers) on 19th December 1914. He was the son of William and Anne Wade and was born on 28th May 1873 in Ballaugh on the Isle of Man. He was married to Kate Wade (born in Coates by Stowe, Lincolnshire in 1877). In 1911 they lived at Biggins Cottages, near Babworth, Retford. At that time they had a son and a daughter, William and Kathleen.

William Wade is buried in All Saints Churchyard, Babworth.

1915

HARRY WRIGHT OSTICK
CH/17306 Royal Marine Light Infantry
Killed 1st January 1915

Retford Times 8th January reports of the death of Harry Wright Ostick, who was on board HMS Formidable when it sank. Harry was the son of Mr and Mrs John Henry Ostick of 25 Water Lane, Retford. Harry Wright Ostick had worked at the Beehive Works when he enlisted in the Royal Marine Light Infantry in 1912.

His parents received a letter from the Admiralty stating that "The name of H W Ostick, who is believed to be on board, does not appear in the list of survivors"; the letter went on to say "Under these circumstances it is feared that unless there is any evidence to the contrary he must be regarded as having lost his life". Harry Wright Ostick was one of 547 men (35 officers and 512 men) to have lost their lives that day out of a complement of 780.

As well as a letter from the Admiralty, a letter was received from Winston Churchill, First Lord of the Admiralty, conveying to the parents the sympathy of the King and Queen.

In 1915 there were ten children in the Ostick family. Sadly, two more were to die in 1917, George, aged twenty-seven, and Fred aged twenty-two.
Harry Ostick has no known grave and is commemorated on the Chatham Naval Memorial.

PRIVATE WILLIAM HENRY REYNOLDS
M2/020592 Army Service Corps (2nd Base Mechanical Transport).
Died 7th January 1915.

Pte William Henry Reynolds died from pneumonia in a hospital in Rouen on 7th January 1915; he was forty-nine. Before enlisting in the Army Service Corp Mechanical Transport he was employed as a chauffeur by Mrs Hunt at Meadowfield. He had three sons, one of whom fought with the Australian Expeditionary Force.

William Reynolds is buried at St. Sever Cemetery, Rouen, France.

DRIVER WALTER EDWARD BLAKE
72615 Royal Field Artillery.
Died 29th January 1915.

Walter Blake was the son of Edward and Louisa Amy Blake, of 35 Trent Street, Retford. He had enlisted only three weeks before he died of pneumonia at the Armstrong College Hospital, Newcastle upon Tyne; he had been ill for just six days. He was twenty-two. Both he and his father Edward had been employed at Merryweather's, the gentlemen's outfitters in Retford. The coffin was carried on a gun carriage to Newcastle Station, accompanied by a firing party; he is buried in East Retford Cemetery.

Private Edward (Ted) Linton Hodson 1392 8th Divisional Cyclist Company, Army Cyclist Corps, formerly 11687 Sherwood Foresters (Notts and Derby Regiment). Killed 9th March 1915.

Edward's father had died and his mother had married James Ryves, living at 33 West Street. He died a day before his brother, Jack, was killed in action.

Edward Hodson was serving with the army in India when war broke out. He was sent to Britain for a month before being posted in France in November 1914. He joined Army Cycling Corps in January 1915.

Edward Hodson has no known grave and is commemorated on the Le Touret Memorial, France.

PRIVATE JOHN WILLIAM (JACK) HODSON
8561 2nd Battalion Lincolnshire Regiment
Killed 10th March 1915.

A report did not reach the Retford Times until July 23rd 1915.
Mr and Mrs Ryves of West Street, Retford received the following by way of the description of the death of their son, Pte John William (Jack) Hodson of the Lincolns, who died fighting for his country on 10th March 1915:

'One morning his regiment was being relieved. I got into conversation with a sergeant and as luck would have it he was Jack's sergeant and he did give him a good character. He said he died a hero's death. It happened one morning when one of Jack's mates was repairing a parapet and the Germans shot him. Jack saw him fall and went to help him and got shot himself. The sergeant did praise him and said what a good lad he was and how he died a hero's death.

Jack's name appears on the Le Touret memorial.

Sadly, Mr and Mrs Ryves lost another son, Private Ted Hodson, of the Army Cyclist Corps. He, like Jack, is remembered on Le Touret Memorial. Another son, John, served as a stoker on HMS Cherwell and survived the War.

PRIVATE WALTER PATTISON

10261 1st Battalion Sherwood Foresters (Notts and Derby Regiment).
Died 12th March 1915.

Pte Walter Pattison was the son of Mr and Mrs Walter Pattison of 44 Tiln Road, Retford. Walter had originally joined the colours in 1906 and had spent six and a half years in India. Walter Pattison's father, also Walter, was employed at Ashworths' Mill, Bolham. He had been working there for over twenty-eight years when news of Walter's death arrived. Prior to this, like Walter Junior, he had been in the army and had also been in India for six years. Pte Walter Pattison died at the Battle of Neuve Chapelle which began on 10th March 1915 with a heavy British artillery barrage on enemy positions at 7.30 a.m. in and around Neuve Chapelle. After thirty-five minutes of bombardment the 23rd and 24th Brigade attacked (the 1St Sherwoods forming part of the 24th Brigade). By 11.00 am on 10th March Neuve Chapelle was in British hands.

The line was held tenuously held through that evening and through all of 11th March. Although being shelled heavily, the 1st Sherwoods were well dug in; despite this, casualties grew during this period. During the night of 11th the Germans were reinforced quite considerably. At 2 p.m. a Company of the 1st Battalion of the Sherwoods attacked with the Royal Scots Fusiliers; making some headway, they found themselves in a trench joining up to derelict farmhouses some 100 to 200 yards from the German line. The troops were greeted with a very misty morning on 12th March and at 5.00 a.m. a German artillery barrage began. This was followed up by an attack by the German Infantry on four points of the front line held by the 1st Sherwoods. The attack came with such ferocity that it swept over the Sherwoods and severe hand-to-hand fighting ensued, with the Battalion falling back on their reserve lines.

The advance of the German attack was checked when heavy rifle fire came from the support trenches, and with the efforts of one of the Company's Bombers, Pte Jacob Rivers (originally from Derby). For his efforts of gallantry Pte Rivers was awarded the Victoria Cross. Pte Rivers was to die in another gallant and brave effort later on that day.

During this action the 1st Sherwoods lost 16 out of 18 officers (9 killed, 7 wounded), 90 other ranks killed and 265 wounded and a further 85 missing. This amounted to 50% of the battalion's strength. Pte Pattison, aged twenty-seven, was a despatch carrier for his company. Sadly, although he was killed on 12th March, his death was not confirmed by the War Office until 17th August, being reported in the Retford Times on 27th August 1915.

A letter from Private C Marsh (Retford lad) says "Just a few lines to let you know that your son Walter has been killed. I suppose you got to know before this. I am sorry for the poor lad. He died doing some splendid work. He was carrying despatches when he was killed."

Both Pte Pattison and Pte Rivers are commemorated on Le Touret Memorial, as they have no known grave.

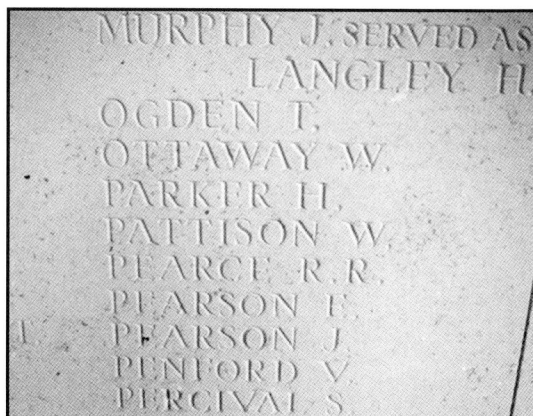

PRIVATE ARTHUR FRARY
2257 1st/8th Battalion Sherwood Foresters (Notts and Derby Regiment).
Killed 12th April 1915

CORPORAL EDGAR HEEDS
9990 1st Battalion York and Lancaster Regiment
Killed 12th April 1915

"In Defence of Right": Retford Times 23rd April 1915.

Under this headline the Retford Times reported the death of two Retford soldiers – one a Regular and the other a Territorial. The regular soldier was Corporal Edgar Heeds, who at the time of his death, serving with the 1st Battalion York and Lancaster's, was just twenty years of age. The territorial soldier serving with the 8th Battalion Sherwood Foresters was Private Arthur Frary.

These two Retford men were good friends before they enlisted in the forces; in fact they lived a few doors away from each other on Ollerton Road and Cpl Heed's sister was engaged to Pte Frary.

Arthur Frary was the youngest of five children. The 1901 Census shows Arthur's father, James, was employed as a railway worker; Herbert and Frederick, Arthur's brothers, were railway engine cleaners; another brother, Harry, was employed as an errand boy; his sister Bertha worked as an apprentice dressmaker, whilst the youngest daughter Alice was described as a scholar.

Pte Frary, serving with the 8th Sherwood Foresters in and around the trenches, was possibly killed whilst working on the trenches during a relief, or may have fallen victim to a German sniper as the History of the Battalion does not report any major action.

Arthur Frary is buried at Kemmel Chateau Military Cemetery, Belgium.

Edgar Heeds was educated at the Council School, Thrumpton. He was also a choirboy at All Hallows Church, Ordsall. He was employed in the offices both at Messrs R. A. Bradshaw and then later at the Retford and Worksop Brewery. Like so many Regulars, Corporal Heeds was based in India when war was declared and was called back immediately. Having spent four days' leave at the beginning of 1915, his battalion were sent to the front in January. His father was employed by Great Northern Railway as the gatekeeper at Babworth Road crossing.

As in many cases, the Heeds family heard of the death of their son before the official news came through. The news was received in the form of a letter from his Company Commander. The letter was as follows: " Dear Mr and Mrs Heeds, I am very sorry to have to tell you that your son's death took place on Monday 12th April (1915), as we were coming from the trenches, having been relieved by another regiment; he was shot straight through the head so he suffered no pain at all. He was buried with several others of the Company near our trench HQ. I shall miss him, as he was a very promising young NCO. Please accept my sincere sympathy in your great loss."

Where Corporal Heeds was buried must have been destroyed in the ensuing fighting, as happened so often. His name is commemorated on the Menin Gate in Ypres, along with 54,323 other servicemen with no known grave, having fought in the Ypres Salient.

SECOND LIEUTENANT JOHN RADLEY EDDISON
'B' Company 8th Battalion Sherwood Foresters
Died 21st April 1915

John Radley Eddison was the son of Robert and Elizabeth Vessey Eddison (Robert was born in Shireoaks. Robert was General Manager for surface and underground mines. John was born Shireoaks. His later schooling was at Giggleswick and he went on to study at Pembroke College.

Before enlisting, John Radley Eddison was a Junior Master at New Beacon School, Sevenoaks. Second Lt Eddison had the misfortune to be the first officer of the 8th Sherwood's to be killed after their arrival in France. According to the Battalion History he was shot whilst out wiring on 21st April 1915. Help was at hand in the form of Drummers Newton and Robb who pulled him out of a shell hole and got him back to the trenches, but he died within minutes.

John Eddison is buried at Kemmel Chateau Military Cemetery, Belgium.

Officers of the 8th Sherwood Foresters at Harpenden in November 1914, including Second Lieutenant John Radley Eddison.

Back row: 2nd Lieut. A. F. O. Dobson, 2nd Lieut. J.S.C. Oates, 2nd Lieut. E.M. Hacking, 2nd Lieut. A. Hacking, 2nd Lieut. W. C. C. Weetman, Lieut. H.B.S. Handford, Capt. J.K. Lane, 2nd Lieut. J. R. Eddison, 2nd Lieut. H. Kirby.

Middle Row: 2nd Lieut. J. M. Gray, 2nd Lieut. W. N. Wright, Lieut. H. G. Wright, 2nd Lieut. B. W. Vann, 2nd Lieut. J. V. Edge, Lieut G. Clarke, 2nd Lieut. W. H. Hollins, 2nd Lieut. E. C. A. James, 2nd Lieut. J. W. Turner, Lieut. C. Davenport.

Fornt Row: Capt. and Qtr.-Mtr. R. F. B. Hodgkinson, Capt. W. H. Allen, Major A. C. Clarke, Rev. J. P. Hales, Capt. and Adjt. E. N. T. Collin, Lieut.-Col. C. J. Huskinson, Major G. H. Fowler, Capt. J. P. Becher, Capt. M. C. Martyn, Capt. A. L. Ashwell, Surgeon-Capt. H. Stallard.

On Ground: 2nd Lieut. R. H. Piggford, 2nd Lieut. A. P. F. Hamilton.

PRIVATE GEORGE WILLIAM TALLENTS
20670 D Company 10th Battalion Alberta Regiment.
Killed 22nd April 1915.

Born in Retford, (his widowed mother lived at 3 Victoria Road), George emigrated to Canada, where he was employed as a Butcher. He was killed in action aged thirty-one years old.

George Tallents has no known grave and is commemorated on the Menin Gate Memorial, Belgium.

'Disastrous News Hits Retford'

This was one of the headlines in the Retford Times and told the story of the death of seven Retfordians killed by the same trench mortar on 24th April 1915.

Private Fred Husband, the brother of Herbert Husband, gave a full account of the incident in which seven Retfordians were killed, in a letter to his parents:

"Just a few lines to let you know poor Herbert was killed last night (April 24th) in action. We were side by side when he was struck in the chest by a trench mortar. I was with him to the last. He did not linger long. It is a wonder any one of us are alive to tell the tale. I shall never forget it as long as I live. We had as far as I can tell 11 killed and a number wounded. It was murder. It was hell itself. I myself was very nearly buried alive, but thank God I was unhurt, but for the shock. I thought my last minutes had come. The scene was terrible. Most of the men had to wade up to their knees in mud and water to get to safety. I was one of those that had to do it to escape being killed. The Lance Corporal over Herbert's section was killed. There were two out of ten left, most of them being Retford lads. Herbert died a true British soldier fighting for his King and Country. I looked after him myself all I could. The officer is writing to you but I thought it best for me to write. Well dear mother and dad, bear up and trust in God".

Private Arthur Parsons, writing to Mrs Grant, the mother of Private Herbert Grant, says: "Just a line to say how I sympathise with you in your great loss. I am pleased to say he stuck to his post while his last. He has been laid to rest in the Sherwood Foresters' burial ground just behind the firing line. I am sure his grave will be looked after whenever we have chance."

Enclosed with the above letter was a note from Lt E C A James: "I am taking the liberty of adding a personal note into this letter, as I am so busy I have not time to write a letter. Your son is buried in the Sherwood Cemetery at Kemmel. Please accept my deep sympathy".

Private Herbert Fisher, a friend of Pte Grant, wrote to Mrs Grant saying: "It is with the greatest regret that I write to tell you that Bert was killed in the trenches on Saturday about 5.30 pm by a shell. I cannot realise it myself. It is too awful. Bert was on sentry duty at the time and stuck to his post like a man. I expect you will have heard from the War Office by the time this arrives, but the news has to be broke. I saw Bert buried in the military cemetery this evening. I cannot write any more; it is too painful."

Another Retford Terrier wrote: "We went into the trenches again on Monday night. The Retford and Newark companies had a very bad time. You will have heard before this letter arrives that seven of the Retford fellows were killed and one very badly wounded. What is known as a trench mortar (a kind of shell that is dropped in the trenches) exploded in their midst. I am sorry to say that amongst the killed were young Hinks of Wharton Street and young Grant of Ollerton Road. You would also be very sorry to hear of the death of Mr Eddison of Mount Vernon. He was shot while in the front of the trench putting up some wire entanglements."

Another young Retford man wrote, "I have some bad news for you at Retford. H. Randall, Hincks, Johnson, Grant, Husband, Pattison and Worthington were all killed on Saturday 24th April. There were some wounded as well. It was murder for the company. I was talking to those (who are now dead) just before they went into the trenches. Young Husband was standing near his brother when he got hit. Some of my mates had to bury them. My God, it is awful to think about."

PRIVATE HERBERT GRANT

2434 1st/8th Battalion Sherwood Foresters (Notts and Derby Regiment).

Pte Herbert Grant was the son of Mr and Mrs Grant of Belvedere, Ollerton Road and was twenty-two years of age when he was killed. He was a native of Ordsall and attended the Council School. He was the last railwayman from Retford to enlist before the authorities stopped railwaymen from joining the colours. He was a point holder on the Great Northern Railway and the youngest of a large family of railway workers. In his last letter Pte Grant wrote: "Just a few lines to let you know that I am still in the best of health and very pleased to hear you are all well at home. It is a beastly job to get a letter off now what with the censors and one thing and another. I wish it was all over".

Herbert Grant is buried at Kemmel Chateau Military Cemetery.

PRIVATE HERBERT HUSBAND

2002 1st/8th Battalion Sherwood Foresters (Notts and Derby Regiment).

Pte Herbert Husband was the youngest son of John and Eliza Husband of 9 Spa Lane. He had three brothers and a brother-in-law who served with His Majesty's forces at the time of his death, aged twenty. His eldest brother, George William Husband, served with the 8th Sherwood Foresters Reserve Battalion at Newton Ferry; he was formerly in the old Notts Volunteers and was a member of the National Reserve. The next brother, Albert, served in the 28th Sherwood Foresters; he also served in the 4th Notts Volunteers. Fred, twenty-two, was in France with the Territorials at the time of his brother's death. He had served four years in the Terriers and prior to his regiment's being mobilised had been employed for eight years as a gardener to Mr R Eddison, Mount Vernon. The deceased's brother-in-law was stationed at South Shields with the Foresters at the time of this disastrous incident.

Herbert Husband is buried at Kemmel Chateau Military Cemetery.

PRIVATE WILLIAM (BILLIE) PATTISON
78 1st/8th Battalion Sherwood Foresters (Notts and Derby Regiment).

"Our representative was informed by Mrs Pattison of Canal Street that she has not yet received any intimation about her son's death but there can be little uncertainty as to his fate. It is said that Private William Pattison had been wounded just before the fatal shell dropped into the trenches and if he could have been removed in time his life might have been saved. He was twenty-four years old and had been employed at the Northern Rubbers Works for eight years and was highly popular amongst his fellow workmen. He was a hardworking official of the Retford Town FC and was a nephew of Sergeant Woodward, the well-known Retford centre-half and who is now attached to the Indian Forces at the front. His brother, Alfred, who is in one of the regular battalions of the Foresters, is a prisoner of war. In the course of a chat with his foreman, Mr O. Appleby, an old Retford cricketer, we learned that "Billie", as his shop-mates knew him, was a pressman in the shoe sole department. He was one of the best workmen, of a genial and happy disposition, and generous to a fault. He was a comrade of Private Frary, who was killed as few weeks ago, also buried at Kemmel Chateau Military Cemetery."

PRIVATE HARRY RANDALL

1839 1st/8th Battalion Sherwood Foresters (Notts and Derby Regiment).

"Mr and Mrs Eli Randall have not received any official intimation of the death of their son, Private Harry Randall. Pte Randall, who was twenty years of age, had been three years in the Territorials and was formerly employed at the Northern Rubber Works."

Harry Randall is buried at Kemmel Chateau Military Cemetery.

PRIVATE WILLIAM JOHNSON

(1867) 1st/8th Battalion Sherwood Foresters (Notts and Derby Regiment).

William Johnson was also employed at the Northern Rubber Works, as was his father. He was twenty-two years of age when he was killed and had been a scholar at the Council School in Retford.

William Johnson is buried at Kemmel Chateau Military Cemetery.

PRIVATE ERNEST WORTHINGTON

(1849) 1st/8th Battalion Sherwood Foresters (Notts and Derby Regiment).

Ernest Worthington was the third son of Mr T Worthington, late of Retford. He sailed to France on his twenty-third birthday. Ernest's brother was with the Reserve Sherwood Foresters stationed at Luton when Ernest died. Their sister was Mrs Lacey of 3, Caledonian Road.

Ernest Worthington is buried at Kemmel Chateau Military Cemetery.

PRIVATE ALBERT EDWARD HINCKS
(1213) 1st/8th Battalion Sherwood Foresters (Notts and Derby Regiment).

Albert Hincks was the only son of Thomas Edward and Harriet Hincks of 40 Wharton Street, Newtown, Retford. He was twenty-three years of age. In a previous issue of the Retford Times it was reported that he had a remarkable escape soon after arriving at the front. A bullet went through his cap and cut through his hair.

Albert Hincks is buried at Kemmel Chateau Military Cemetery.

Extract from the History of 1/8th Sherwood Foresters:

''April 24th witnessed our first serious bombardment. We had already had several somewhat severe baptisms, but they were trifling in comparison. About 6 pm, after an exceptionally quiet day, and just before we were to be relieved, the enemy began an organised trench mortar bombardment of G1 and G2 (trenches), occupied by platoons of C and D companies, and H4 held by Lt. Vann and his platoon of B Company. It lasted for about an hour, and made large breaches in the parapet of G1 and 2, and practically demolished the whole of H4, a small isolated trench on the extreme left, opposite Petit Bois. Both these trenches were completely enfiladed by the Boche, so that their shooting was extremely accurate. It was thought at one time that the enemy might attempt a raid on G1 and G2, but this did not develop.

A machine gun team consisting of L/Cpl Sharrock and Ptes Hopewell and Davis, which was posted in G1, behaved most coolly, and Sgt A Phillipson of D company did very gallant work in the same trench under heavy fire with Pte Coombes and Durand, all in a more or less dazed condition, helping to dig out the wounded. On the left, Vann and his platoon had a very bad time. Whilst he was digging out the wounded a bomb fell close by, killing four and burying three others, and blowing Vann himself several yards across the open at the back of the trench, and practically wiping out the garrison.

Major Becher brought up reinforcements and helped Vann to get the position made good, and great assistance was given by 2nd Lt Hollins and L/Cpl Humberstone. Ptes F Boothby and A Gleaden of B Company also did excellent work, helping to dig out and dress the wounded, most of the time in full view of the enemy, not more than 70 yards away. The 2nd Royal Scots on our immediate left also gave us valuable assistance.

Our total casualties during the hours bombardment were 14 men killed and two Officers Vann and Gray and 14 men wounded.

The dead were:
Pte Hunt, Pte Redmile, Pte Godfrey, Pte Hibbert, Pte East, Pte Bonner, Pte Grant,

Pte Husband, Pte Johnson, Pte Pattison, L Cpl Ashley, Pte Hincks, Pte Randall, Pte Worthington."

The seven other Sherwood Foresters killed in the incident are listed below:

LANCE CORPORAL WILLIAM WALTON ASHLEY
(2174) was the son of Mr. and Mrs. J. W. Ashley, of Shrublands, South Park, Lincoln; he was aged twenty-three.

PRIVATE WALTER HUNT
(1396) aged 20, son of George and Martha Hunt, of 31, Grove St., New Balderton, Newark.

PRIVATE CHARLES REDMILE
(864) aged 27, brother of Mrs. R. E. M. Matthews, of 42, Vernon St., Newark.

PRIVATE WILLIAM GODFREY
(879) aged 22, son of William Henry and Annie Elizabeth Godfrey, of 41, Bowbridge Rd., Newark, aged twenty-two.

PRIVATE CHARLES HENRY HIBBERT
(2200) aged 22, son of Joseph and Mary Ann Hibbert, of 54, Princes St., Mansfield.

PRIVATE RICHARD EAST
(2133) aged 23, son of the late Richard Cartwright East and Fanny Louisa East, of Newark.

PRIVATE JAMES BONNER
(1093) aged 28, son of John and Elizabeth Bonner, of Brant Broughton, Newark.

LANCE CORPORAL CECIL LAND

2249 8th Battalion Sherwood Foresters (Notts and Derby Regiment).
Killed 2nd May 1915.

On 7th May 1915 news was received of the death of Lance Corporal Cecil Land, a nephew of Mrs Dallas and Miss Howlee of Holly Road, also of the 8th Sherwood Foresters (Territorials). The brave young man, who was only nineteen, was hit by a stray bullet 2nd May. He was an old Retford Grammar School boy. He is buried in Loker churchyard, West-Vlaanderen, Belgium.

Cecil Land enlisted in the 1/8th Sherwood (Notts. and Derby Regiment) in 1914 at Newark where the Battalion was formed. He was a private in 'C' Company.

Cecil was born in Paris in 1896; his parents were George and Edith Land. Cecil was the nephew of W. J. Jenkins (of Jenkins fame).

The 18th September 1914 edition of the Retford Times reports that the 1/8th Sherwood Foresters set off from Newark at 9.45 am on 14th September 1914 for foreign service. Cecil left Newark in the company of three other Old Retfordians, namely David Tanner, son of Councillor David Tanner (his brother Harold was also with the Battalion), Robert Plant, son of Mr Plant of Dominie Cross, and Sydney Lister, son of Mrs Lister of Westfields. Sadly, all of these Old Retfordians were to die in action, except Harold Tanner.

A report a week later, the Retford Times reported that the Battalion were encamped at Mountford in the Thames Valley. It was to be a further five months before the Battalion left for foreign shores and even then it was not to be a smooth mobilisation.

The Battalion diary reports that on 25th February 1915 31 officers and 996 other ranks embarked on the SS Mount Temple from Southampton. The Battalion now formed part of 139th Brigade 46th (Midland Division). Having left the port, the ship proceeded to anchor off Netley for the night. The following day they returned to Southampton where 21 officers and 763 other ranks disembarked and proceeded to a rest camp on the outskirts of Southampton. On 28th February 1915 Captain Becher, along with 101 other ranks, embarked on the SS Caledonian for France. The rest of the Battalion left later in the day for France aboard the SS King Edward. This detachment, however, was ordered to disembark again and billeted at Watt Memorial Hall, Southampton. This detachment finally sailed for France on 2nd March 1915.

Having landed at Le Havre on 3rd March, the Battalion entrained for Cassel on 4th March and then marched to their billets at Oudezeele. While they were in their billets, Captain Becher's detachment arrived, having spent three days on the SS Caledonian.

After spending five days in billets, the Battalion then spent the next four days marching from Merris to Cassel via Caëstre and Strazelee (9th March). The following day (10th March) the battalion were marched to Bac St. Maur via La Rouge Croix. Following several route marches the Battalion found itself under the 10th Brigade, 4th Division, and receiving instruction in trench war at Ploegsteert and opposite Messines towards the end of March.

At the beginning of April, Cecil Land found himself in trenches near Kemmel with the Battalion resting at Locre when out of the line. At this point the trenches were between 25 and 300 yards, being closest at an area near Peckham Corner.

On Easter Day 1915 there was an attempt at a truce, with Germans showing the white flag. Whilst there was conversation between the opposing forces there was no fraternisation on the scale of Christmas 1914 in certain sectors. All conversation ceased with sniper fire, resulting in a number of soldiers being shot, the first being Pte Jack Hyde, aged eighteen, from Daybrook in Nottingham, who is buried at Kemmel Chateau Military Cemetery, where several natives of Retford are also buried.

The Summer 1915 edition of The Retfordian Magazine (the Retford Grammar School termly publication) reported:

"Relatives in Retford have received some most comforting and sympathetic letters from comrades and officers of his regiment. He is buried at Locrew (Locre) not far from Ypres and the number of his grave is greater than 100. So he is not alone".

CORPORAL GEORGE WILLIAM INGALL
32518 5th Oxford and Bucks Light Infantry, formerly 1866 Sherwood Foresters (Notts and Derby Regiment).
Killed 3rd May 1915.

George William Ingall as a Private in the Sherwood Foresters. Above his right tunic pocket is the Imperial Service Badge indicating his willingness to serve abroad

George originally served with the 1/8th Battalion Sherwood Foresters and arrived in France during June 1915 (in the 1st draft/reinforcement to the Battalion). His regimental number makes him a pre-1914 enlistment - probably mid-1913. George was born in Gainsborough, Lincolnshire, but enlisted in Retford.

George's Battalion was attached to the 14th (Light) Division when it took part in the Third Battle of the Scarpe, one of the actions which made up the Battle of Arras. The 5th Oxford and Bucks attacked Hillside Work (Vis-en-Artois) on 3rd May 1915. Out of the 12 officers and 523 NCO's and other ranks, 8 officers and 291 other ranks became casualties. It was during this action that George Ingall was killed.

George Ingall has no known grave and is commemorated on the Arras Memorial, France.

PRIVATE FRANK PICKARD
2188 Nottinghamshire Yeomanry (Sherwood Rangers).
Died 6th May 1915.

Frank Pickard was employed at Jenkins prior to joining the Sherwood Rangers in October 1914. His parents, Harry (born 1854 in Retford) and Sally Pickard (born 1850 in Billinghay, Lincs) lived at 151 Moorgate Hill, Retford. Frank's father was well known in the town and worked for the Town Clerks Department. Special mention of Frank's death was made at a Council Meeting.

Having trained at Sheringham in Norfolk, Frank embarked for Egypt in 1915. He was apparently kicked by a horse and, having been hospitalised in Alexandria, died, aged twenty-three, from his injuries on board the HMS Goorkha. He was buried at sea and is commemorated on the Helles Memorial.

Frank had a brother, Charles, in the Sherwood Rangers, and another brother, Thomas, who returned from South America to serve with the Royal Engineers.

PRIVATE SIDNEY MILLER

15030 1st Battalion Sherwood Foresters (Notts and Derby Regiment).
Killed 9th May 1915.

Sidney Miller was one of the many young men who enlisted having left his employment at Messrs W J Jenkins and Co. He enlisted in the army in September 1914 and there then followed a long period of training. Sidney did not embark for France until March 26th 1915. It is most likely that Sidney, along with 223 other ranks, joined the 1st Sherwoods following their heavy losses at Neuve Chapelle in March 1915. It was on 9th May 1915 that the 8th Division, of which the 1st Sherwoods were part (24th Brigade), were involved in the Battle of Aubers Ridge. The attack was in support of an attack being undertaken by the French. There were to be attacks in and around Aubers, one to the north in which Sidney Miller would have been involved, and an attack to the south.

The Sherwoods marched out from their billets near Sailly on 8th April 1915, arriving at their assembly trenches near Petillon just after midnight with very little mishap. The attack was to be against Rouges Bancs with a start time of 5.30 a.m., following a short but heavy artillery bombardment. Initially the attack was undertaken by 25th Brigade but with heavy losses being sustained and very little or no progress being made, the 2nd East Lancashires and 'B' and 'D' company of the Sherwoods joined the attack at 5.55 am. Coming under heavy machine gun fire, the attack was called off and the troops retired to trenches that lay behind. At 7.35 a.m. an attack was called for, and this time it involved all four companies of the 1st Battalion Sherwood Foresters and the East Lancashires. Again this advance was checked by machine gun fire with many men lying down where they had advanced to. Those who made it back to their start-off trenches came under high explosive bombardments following a lull at about 7.30 p.m., and a large number of casualties were sustained. The Battalion was finally relieved at 10 pm by the Worcestershire Regiment, arriving back near Rouge de Bout at 1.00 a.m.

Sidney Miller has no known grave and is commemorated on the Ploegsteert Memorial, Belgium.

PRIVATE JOHN DISTANCE HILTON

11062 1st Sherwood Foresters (Notts and Derby Regiment).
Died 14th May 1915.

On 21st May 1915 news of the death of another Retfordian who had enlisted in the Sherwood Foresters reached Retford. The deceased soldier was Private John Distance Hilton, son of Mr and Mrs Hilton of 28 Beehive Street. He died on 14th May 1915 at Le Touquet from wounds received in action (see Sidney Miller, above). John Hilton had most likely been wounded in the same action, as he died on 9th May. The parents received the first notification of their son's being wounded in the following letter from a friend, Private F Smallwood: " I am sorry to tell you of your son's accident, but I told Jack if anything happened to him I would let you know as soon as is possible. Jack was cook with me and I can tell you I miss him. The men always thought a lot of him. The wound that Jack received was not serious, but I will expect it will take him home to England. Jack has been a chum of mine about six years and I miss him. I am very sorry for him and hope he will soon recover." Like so many others, he received a wound not thought serious but which could become life-threatening in a short period of time. On the Saturday night, after the arrival of the letter outlined above, Mrs Hilton received a telegram from the officer in charge stating, "It is with regret that I have to inform you that No. 11062 Private John Hilton, 1st Notts and Derbys, died at 10.50 14th May at a Canadian Stationary Hospital, Le Touquet".

Pte Hilton, who was twenty-six years of age, enlisted in the Foresters in 1909, serving as a regular in India. He returned to England in October 1914 and after four days' visit to Retford went to the Front with his Regiment. Prior to enlistment he was employed by Mr Peck of Bothamsall.

John Hilton is buried in Le Touquet-Paris Plage Communal Cemetery, France.

LIEUTENANT ARTHUR MARSHALL OAKDEN
Royal Marine Engineers.
Died 21st May 1915.

Arthur Marshall was the son of William and Mary Oakden, whose address on the 1901 census was given as Bank House, Retford. William was employed as a bank manager. Arthur was a pupil at the Retford Grammar. He went on to study at Manchester University and was a Whitworth Exhibitioner (ie his work was put on display at the Whitworth Gallery in Manchester). He was also a student of the Institute of Civil Engineering. For three years he was a member of the East Lancs Territorials R.E., and later a member of the OTC at Manchester University, enlisting in September 1914.

Arthur Marshall Oakden was a Lieutenant in the 1st Field Company Division Engineers, Royal Naval Division, Royal Marine Engineers (later to become 247th Field Company). Arthur was gazetted on 1st January 1915 to the post of Temporary Lieutenant, which, however, had taken effect from 26th October 1914.

On 25th April 1915 the landings began at Gallipoli, the Royal Marine, including Arthur's

No 1 Field Company of the Divisional Engineers, landed in the first few days. They remained at Anzac Bay from 28th April to 13th May 1915. On 13th May the Royal Marines were returned to Helles, landing at W beach (Lancashire Landing). The Brigade remained here from 14th May to 24th May. It was whilst bivouacking here that Arthur was very likely to have been killed during continuous shelling that took place daily. Douglas Jerrold in his 'History of the Royal Naval Division' states: "losses in specific operations were miraculously few, the daily wastage from shells in the camps and trenches was high." Jerrold lists the officer casualties, including that of Lt. Arthur Marshall Oakden of the Divisional Engineers at the age of twenty-six.

Report in Retford Times June 6th 1915
Memorial Service for Retford Officer.

"On Monday last there was a special service in the memory of Arthur Marshall Oakden of the Engineers Section of the Royal Naval Division who, as recorded in our last edition, died of wounds received during operations. The service was held in the Parish Church of St Swithun's, with which the deceased officer has been intimately connected for many years.

In addition to a large number of relatives, a large congregation of friends and sympathisers had assembled. The staff and a large number of pupils from Retford Grammar School, where Lt. Oakden had been educated, were present. The officiating clergy were the Vicar (The Rev J T Mumford) and the Headmaster of the Grammar School, the Reverend T Gough. The beautiful Psalm XC was sung to a setting by Keeton and the hymns were "The Saints of God Their Conflicts Past" and "On the Resurrection Morn". At the close of what had been a most moving service, "God Save the King" was sung, followed by Chopin's Marche Funebre on the organ.
Universal sympathy is felt for Mr and Mrs Oakden in the loss of their gallant son, as for so many others who have lost their boys in obedience to the call of King and Fatherland"

Arthur Oakden is buried in Lancashire Landing Cemetery, Gallipoli, Turkey.

PRIVATE ALFRED PATTERSON
14650 1st Battalion Lincolnshire Regiment.
Killed 16th June 1915

Aged only seventeen when he died, Alfred Patterson's father had served in the Boer War, so it would have seemed natural for him to join up. Alfred was killed during the Battle of Bellewaarde, a follow-up to the 2nd Battles of Ypres. On the day that he died more than 4,000 men would be casualties on a field half a mile square.

Alfred Patterson has no known grave and is commemorated on the Menin Gate Memorial, Belgium.

PRIVATE GEORGE WILLIAM (WILLIE) TINKER
1972 1st/8th Battalion Sherwood Foresters.
Killed 16th July 1915.

In the Retford Times the death of Pte Willie Tinker of the 8th Sherwood Foresters was announced. George, who was the grandson of Mrs Tinker of the Cricketers' Arms, Retford, was killed in action on 16th July 1915. Pte Tinker, who had celebrated his eighteenth birthday on 4th June 1915, was described as being cheerful and "very popular amongst his chums." George had been in France only three weeks and in the trenches five days when a rifle grenade killed him. Mrs Tinker 's first intimation of his death was through a letter sent by Pte George Ostick (also to be a casualty of the war, in 1917), who described himself as"a very close chum of the brave soldier. " George Ostick was wounded in the same action. Pte Tinker had been a scholar at the National School and on leaving was employed at Messrs W. J. Jenkins and Son.

In a letter to Mrs Tinker, Lieutenant Colonel Fowler, Commanding Officer (who became a victim during the battle of Loos 1915), says: "I am sorry to have to write and tell you that your grandson Private Tinker was killed in the trenches Thursday last by a rifle grenade sent by the Germans. The trench he was in was very close to their lines and consequently they bombarded us with these explosive things very much. I do want you to understand how sorry I am for you in your great trouble. The only consolation is that he has died a soldier's death for his King and Country's sake. He was buried in the wood behind the trenches and the grave will be marked."

A friend in another letter wrote to Mrs Tinker stating, "I wish to express my deepest sympathy in your great loss. I can assure you he died doing his duty for his King and Country. He died at his post. It is a great blow to all who knew him. Every hour that passes I shall think of his dear face for he was always so quiet and happy. The other day we heard a buzzer like Jenkins and he said he wished he were going to work. God bless him and look after him. I am sure he will be greatly missed by us all. I cannot say much for his absence preys on my mind. With all our deepest sympathy."

Willie Tinker is buried in Sanctuary Wood Cemetery, Belgium.

HAROLD WATERFIELD
10679 6th Battalion Lincolnshire Regiment.
Drowned 23rd July 1915.

On 16th August 1915 a memorial service was held to remember Harold Waterfield, who sadly and tragically was drowned accidentally whilst serving in the Dardanelles. A large congregation gathered in West Retford Church, where the pulpit and stall were draped in black in memory of Harold. The service was delivered by Mr John Ward of the United Methodist Church. The preacher expressed deep sympathy to the family in their loss and referred to the numbers who had passed through the Sunday Schools of the country, and specific mention was made of the sixteen with the forces who were connected with the Retford Baptists, of whom fourteen were members of the Sunday School. He also stated that Harold was the second to lose his life, the first being Albert Hincks who was one of seven killed by the same bomb in April 1915.

Harold, who was only eighteen years old when he died, had two other brothers serving with the Sherwood Rangers at the time of his death. His mother, Liza Turner lived at 62 Moorgate Retford.

Harold Waterfield is buried in Lancashire Landing Cemetery, Gallipoli, Turkey.

PRIVATE JOHN ROSSINGTON
2256 1st/8th Battalion Sherwood Foresters (Notts and Derby Regiment).
Killed 30th July 1915.

John Rossington was the son of Lucy and John Rossington of West Street.

The death of Pte John Rossington of the 8th Sherwood Foresters, who was killed on 30 July 1915, was announced in the Retford Times dated 6th August 1915. The following week in the Retford Times a letter was printed received by Mrs F R Rossington (John's wife) of 8 Whitehall Road, Retford. The letter, sent by Pte G G Gilbert, gave particulars of how the "gallant soldier met his death." Pte Rossington was in the Sanctuary Wood Trench System when he was killed.

The letter stated: "It must be a terrible blow for you

to learn of the death of your husband. He was shot through the head whilst out at a listening post about 11.00 on Friday evening 29thJuly. It was I think impossible for him to have been seen so it must have been quite a chance shot. It was very sudden and he never spoke. He became unconscious immediately and by the time I arrived at the scene he was dead. He is buried with other men of the Battalion who have fallen in a wood quite close behind the firing line and his grave will have a wooden cross on it. None of his friends from his company were able to go to his funeral as they could not be spared from the trenches, but we shall be able to go and see his grave before long. To us here it was a great shock. No one in No 11 Platoon was more reliable or more ready to do anything pleasant and unpleasant than your husband. He was liked by all the men and his gap will be very much felt indeed. He was a man I shall never forget. He has entered the company of those who have sacrificed all they had for the sake of what they hold to be right and I am sure you will look back on this end with pride for no death could be nobler. Our deepest sympathy is with you in your great trouble and we pray you will have the strength to bear it."

John Rossington has no known grave and is commemorated on the Menin Gate Memorial, Ypres, Belgium.

LANCE CORPORAL EDWIN HUTCHINSON TAYLOR
657 4th Battalion Australian Infantry, A.I.F..
Died between the 6th and 9th August 1915.

Edwin Hutchinson, born on 17th September 1891, in Bangalore, India, was the son of Dr Vincent O and Maria Jane Taylor. At the time of his death his parents lived at Trevons, High Street, Selsey, Sussex. Edwin was the grandson of Edwin Wilmhurst, a prominent businessman in Retford, owning an ironmongery shop at 56 Bridgegate, Retford. It would appear that there were strong links with Sussex as Edwin Wilmhurst was born there. Edwin was to travel twice to India and back before the age of eight. The 1901 Census reveals that Edwin Hutchinson Taylor, aged nine, was visiting his grandfather (aged sixty-eight in 1901) with his mother (aged forty in 1901). Information suggests that Edwin was of a frail nature and suffered with health problems from the age of twelve to twenty-one.

Edwin Hutchinson Taylor attended the Grammar School in Retford and boarded with his grandfather on Bridgegate. Taylor was described as being "very delicate". It would appear from records that he was keen on all Natural History, especially that of jungles. It is therefore not surprising that Edwin Taylor found work with a company in British East Africa (the territory included the now-independent countries of Tanzania (formerly Tanganyika and the island of Zanzibar), Kenya, and Uganda. Whilst in BEA, Taylor suffered a serious illness and was advised to "take a voyage" by doctors. The voyage took him to Australia.

While at school Edwin penned the following lines in 1902 when he was just eleven:

> The world is like a tailor shop
> Where overcoats you buy
> And you are sent in to the world
> To lead good lives - and then die.
>
> But death is not a horrible thing
> As many folk suppose
> But only casting off
> Of your worn-out clothes
>
> *Edwin Hutchinson Taylor*

Having sailed from Australia in October 1914, the Australian Expedition Force arrived in Egypt in December and started training in and around Mena, just outside Cairo in sight of the Pyramids.

In a letter to the school dated 13th May 1915 Taylor writes about forming part of a picket at a town called Karsr-el-Nil in Egypt and mentions being "there through the riots when red caps (Military Police) shot several Australians and Territorials". Following this incident, Taylor writes that they were "soon taken off picket and sent to Mena to get ready for the Front".

In preparation, the Battalion sailed from Alexandria to the Isle of Lemnos where they stayed for two weeks, practising amphibious landings. On 25th April 1915, following a "stealthy cruise", the various brigades landed at a number of different points, about which Taylor goes on to write "I cannot tell you particulars much as I would like to". Having struck a "hot spot", Taylor's battalion drove the Turks from their trench and they went on to experience a mixture of 'shrapnel, machine gun fire and land rifle fire, also Turks and Germans in Australian rig. On the Tuesday after the landing Taylor was wounded, but was able to walk to a dressing station and from there taken by Transporter back to Egypt, taking four days to reach there. Taylor then had an operation "under chloroform to have some loose bits of flesh and bone removed", and continued to write that he was doing well on a full diet and expected to be back with his battalion within the month.

Below is an excerpt from a diary written by John Gibson Pitt 8th Battalion AIF, which may also have been referring to the incident described by Hutchinson Taylor:

April 2nd 1915
Church parade 9 a.m. in Red X hall. Good sermon by Capt Dexter. Rumours of our departure on Monday and so I should take the opportunity of having a look at Heliopolis (a suburb of Cairo) where the 2nd contingent of New Zealanders is camped. There is a splendid service of electric trams, they start on the road and then follow alongside

the railway line for a couple of miles and out to the road again.On our way back we saw countless millions of locusts, they are just like huge clouds. Arrived back in Cairo about 3 o'clock and at 4 o'clock, being near one of the lowest streets in Cairo, and noticing a big crowd there, investigated, only to find that a quarrel had arisen between some of the New Zealanders and the natives, with the result that the former went into the houses and entirely cleared them out, throwing everything in to the street, a piano included, and setting fire to it, soon there was a large bonfire in the middle of the street. After a while about 20 of the Redcaps (M.M.P) arrived on the scene and when in the middle of the crowd, they were greeted with lumps of limestone chairs etc, with the result that the redcaps drew their revolvers and fired on the crowd, about 10 shots were fired, in addition to a few from our fellows who chanced to have revolvers. Two or three were wounded. About 5 o'clock a platoon of L F's (Lancashire Fusiliers) arrived and half an hour later a squadron of Westminster Dragoons. The Fire Brigade turned out, but they were put to flight by the crowd, the hose cut in halves and a half deposited at each end of the street. More dragoons and infantry arrived later, also the Australasian Provost Marshall, who made an appeal to all those men that wished to help him to clear the street, and were not interested in the affair, to return to camp. Barney Allan and I returned, as asked. Arrived back in camp about 9 pm.

Letter from Edwin H Taylor 4th Battalion Australian Infantry received by Rev. T. Gough on 14th August 1915.

"I have been back here a month now and have been in the trenches nearly all the time. Today I am in the open with 15 others to guard a barricade; so I managed to get a few sheets of letter paper from a friend… Although a man can write from here, all letters are strictly censored, so I can say nothing of interest about conditions, facts or rumours. I am sorry my letters got a bit soiled in writing; but you can guess what it is like here; thermometer over 100, dry dusty soil in the trenches, dust and flies everywhere, one pint of water a day, sleep in boots, never wash week in week out. Not too good, but much better than it might be.

The nights are cool - almost cold and certainly as yet we have not had to sleep in pools of water with mud for a pillow. We are daily in expectation of the gas-racket here and have respirator equipment always handy. The country however is so broken and full of nullahs (ravines) that the wind which is very changeable on its own account is most uncertain in blowing through the, and the Turks; I think they are afraid to start gassing for fear it should blow back on themselves. We are not engaged in any hot action here just now, but sitting in trenches and keeping a sharp look-out.

The Turks have some remarkably good marksmen amongst them: should a man on observation keep his periscope up for a few seconds too long at a time he gets a bullet smack through the middle of it and the top mirror gets knocked down in splinters into the eyes... The Turkish bullets have a very thin nickel coating on them, and when they strike stone or hard earth, sparks fly off. The Turks are generally using the practice of reversing their bullets; this causes very bad wounds when a man is hit. On the whole, since our Govt. threatened to hold their leaders personally responsible, they are fighting pretty fair; they do not, for example, shell the hospital ships. We get tobacco issued once a week and rum and lime juice occasionally. Our only real hardship is loss of sleep."

Sadly this was Edwin Taylor's last letter and in fact reached the head teacher, Rev. Thomas Gough, over a week after Taylor was killed in action at Lone Pine on the Gallipoli peninsula, his date of death being given as between 6th and 9th August 1915. He is buried in Johnston's Jolly Cemetery, Gallipoli.

Four Killed by Shell
Retford Times August 1915

In August, 8th Battalion of the Sherwood Foresters (Notts and Derby Regiment) suffered another disaster, four of their company being killed by a shell. The Retford Times states that the "distressing news was received in the Town on Thursday week that four members of the 8th Battalion Sherwood Foresters had been killed on the previous Monday morning". The report goes on to state that they were Sergeant Phillipson, Lance Corporal Scott (both of Richard Street, Newtown), Private Ernest King, and Private Albert Smith. The report ends with "the deepest sympathy of the townspeople is extended to the parents of the deceased in their great bereavement".

SERGEANT ARTHUR PHILLIPSON
8 1st/8th Battalion Sherwood Foresters (Notts and Derby Regiment).
Killed 8th August 1915.

The death, under the headline "Sergeant Arthur Phillipson", was reported on the same page in the Retford Times as the brief report outlined above. Sgt Arthur Phillipson, who was thirty-two at the time of his death, was the second son of Mr and Mrs George Phillipson of Richard Street, Newtown, Retford. Arthur, like so many, had joined the Retford Volunteer Company in 1905. With hard work and perseverance in his duties Arthur reached the rank of Sergeant in the Volunteer Company. He was described as being "of a quiet and genial disposition and took great interest in his work". Having attended Thrumpton Lane School, he was first employed in the gardens of The Elms (now a hotel), which at the time of his employment was the home of Alderman J W Holmes. He then moved jobs and was employed at Northern Rubbers until enlisting with the colours. Arthur must have been one of the first to join, as his regimental number was 8.

In the report reference was made to the incident on 24th April 1915, when a shell killed seven Retford members of the battalion, and that Sgt Phillipson's platoon paid a tribute of praise to him for his brave deed performed in the trenches. Praise was also forthcoming from Lieutenant Jones, Sgt Phillipson's superior: he stated in a letter that "he was proud to have such a sergeant under him."

In the The Sherwood Foresters in the Great War 1914-1919 8th Battalion written by Captain W C Weetman, Sgt Phillipson is mentioned on three occasions: once during the attack on 24th April 1915 in which seven Retfordians were killed by one shell. The book states that on that fateful day "Sergeant A Phillipson of 'D' Company did very gallant work" in the trenches when under heavy fire. The second occasion was during the attack in early August which resulted in the death of four more Retfordians, including Sgt Phillipson. The book goes on to tell us that, holding the left of the line, the position was uncertain, and "Sergeant A. Phillipson in particular, in command of the left platoon No. 13, had a most anxious and trying time"; the book goes on to say that the accounts given "might easily have demoralised our Battalion but for the magnificent example of Lieut. James, his second-in-command, 2nd Lieut. Vann, and Sergeant A Phillipson and the coolness and courage of every man in 'D' Company." The third mention states that 36 other ranks were killed and wounded, including Sgt Phillipson, "who throughout had shewn the utmost coolness and gallantry".

It was for this action that Sgt Phillipson was mentioned in Sir John French's final despatch in November 1915, along with 6000 other men and officers.

It would appear that "a little girl", who made a number of articles and sold them, the money going towards writing materials, adopted Sergeant Arthur Phillipson. Sadly, the "little girl's" identity remains a mystery. The article in the Retford Times states that Sergeant Phillipson acknowledged the materials and that "the men are very pleased with the paper, envelopes and pencils," and how he was "proud" of the fact that "someone so young was working on our behalf." He went on to say that he would send "a few postcards which I hope you will like". He remarked that the weather was "lovely here and if it were not for the terrible war I should be enjoying myself." He signed off the letter "Your Soldier Friend."

Arthur Phillipson is buried in Sanctuary Wood Cemetery, Belgium.

LANCE CORPORAL PERCY SCOTT

1676 1st/8th Battalion Sherwood Foresters (Notts and Derby Regiment).
Killed 8th August 1915.

Lance Corporal Percy Scott, aged nineteen, was the only son of Mr and Mrs Joseph Scott of 18 Richard Street, Newtown, Retford. Like so many Retfordians, Percy was a member of the Retford Territorials and had attended two summer camps before the outbreak of war, his last being at Filey. The Scotts were sent a letter from Pte Frank Farrand (to be killed at the Battle of Loos later in the year).

Outlining the circumstances of the death of their son and the three others, the letter said, "I am writing to you with deep regret to inform you that poor Percy got killed on Monday morning along with three more lads by a shell. It all occurred in this way. Two Battalions on the left of our company were to make an attack at dawn. After an hour's bombardment of the of the German trenches, those on our left attacked the trenches in front so our company had to file down into the trench they had left, and so came in for a good deal of shell fire. I am very sorry to say it was while we were holding this trench that Percy and the three other lads were killed. I was in the next bay, and got a good shaking but am pleased to say nothing more".

Percy Scott is buried in Sanctuary Wood Cemetery, Belgium.

PRIVATE ERNEST KING

1216 1st/8th Battalion Sherwood Foresters (Notts and Derby Regiment).
Killed 8th August 1915.

Pte Ernest King was the only son of Mr and Mrs Ambrose King of Fenton Villas, Dominie Cross Road, Retford. Before enlisting, he was employed at the Beehive Engineering works where his father also worked. He had actually been in the Territorials for some three years when he was killed at the age of twenty-one. In the report in the Retford Times announcing his death, his father in an interview said, "It is very hard to lose an only son, but we have the consoling fact that he died in action doing his duty; and our hope is that the splendid sacrifice Britain is making will not be in vain."

Like Sgt Phillipson, Ernest had received some of the writing materials from a "little girl". In a letter to her he wrote "The Retford boys are pleased to think how our little friends have still got us in mind."

Also in the letter there was a touch of patriotism when he wrote "This war is a struggle England has never seen before, but I can say we are winning". An indirect message was given to those back at home who had not enlisted when he also wrote "Everything is going well, and if the lads at home answer the call, as they are doing, the Germans will be sure to give way before long." In his letter home Ernest gave some idea of trench life by saying that "The other night the bounders attacked us at night at one point, blowing up three mines. But we stuck to it and they were repulsed with murderous fire from our rifles and machine guns."

Ernest King has no known grave and is commemorated on the Menin Gate, Ypres, Belgium.

PRIVATE ALBERT SMITH
1966 1st/8th Battalion Sherwood Foresters (Notts and Derby Regiment).
Killed 8th August 1915.

Albert Smith was the fourth member of the 8th Sherwood Foresters to be killed on that terrible day in August 1915. Albert was the eldest son of Mr and Mrs Henry Smith of Alma Road, Retford. Like so many, Smith was killed while in the prime of life: he was only twenty years old. Smith was also one of the growing numbers of men who were being killed at the front having been employed at Messrs Jenkins and Co Ltd before enlisting. A letter from Pte George Sly, son of Mr Alan Sly of Woolpack Street, again outlined the circumstances in which Albert Smith was killed. The letter states that "He was buried in nice burial ground at the back of the firing line and you can rest assured that his grave will be well looked after". Sadly this was not the case as Albert Smith is remembered on the Menin Gate, along with the other soldiers who died in the Ypres Salient and have no known grave.

PRIVATE GEORGE SPRAY
10700 6th Battalion Lincolnshire Regiment.
Killed 9th August 1915.

Private James Spray 13229 9th Battalion Sherwood Foresters (Notts and Derby Regiment).
Killed 9th August 1915.

The 1911 Census shows George and James Spray living with their grandmother, Caroline McMillan, a widow who owned a newsagent at 44 Carolgate. George was employed as a moulder whilst younger brother James assisted in his grandmother's business.

The 6th Lincolns and the 9th Sherwood Foresters both took part in an amphibious landing at Sulva Bay on the 7th August 1915, in a final attempt to break the deadlock in the Battle of Gallipoli. Two days later the brothers were dead.

The circumstances surrounding the brothers' deaths are not known, but fate decided that both would die in the same place, on the same day, despite serving in different regiments.

George Spray and James Spray have no known graves and are commemorated on the Helles Memorial, Gallipoli, Turkey.

PRIVATE ALFRED HEWITT
10693 6th Battalion Lincolnshire Regiment.
Killed 9th August 1915.

Before enlisting, Pte Hewitt, son of Alfred and Martha Hewitt, lived at 79 Mount Pleasant, Spital Hill, Retford with his parents. Alfred enlisted on 1st September 1914 and was killed on 9th August 1915. His family was first notified by several letters arriving from the Dardanelles to relatives of other soldiers. One such writer was Pte Horace Cartwright of the same Regiment, who wrote to his own mother, of Long Row, Spital Hill, saying "We have had some severe fighting this weekend and have lost a good many men. Alf Hewitt was killed on August 8th [actually 9th] and I think Harry Smith has been wounded but Leonard is alright. (a later letter from Pte. Footitt stated differently). The fighting was like hell. No one would have believed it if they had not seen it. We never had a wash for about a week; it was awful." Pte Cartwright also wrote to a Mrs Durham of St John Street, Retford, outlining the same information.

Further evidence of Alfred's death came via a letter dated 12th August 1915 from Pte. Fred Footitt to his mother, who also lived on Spital Hill. In his letter Fred Footitt said that "We have lost a lot of men and have only about 150 men left out of our battalion which was 1200 at the outset. We have only four of five officers left … I have not seen young Len Smith or Alfred Hewitt. I think they have gone under." In a letter sent dated 14th August 1915, Fred Footitt wrote saying that Alfred Hewitt had been killed.

Alfred Hewitt has no known grave and is commemorated on the Helles Memorial, Gallipoli.

CORPORAL WALTER HOLEY
10716 6th Battalion Lincolnshire Regiment.
Killed 9th August 1915.

Walter Holey was born in 1897, his parents being Walter and Eleanor Holey. Walter Snr came from Brayton, Yorkshire, and records show he was born about 1858. Eleanor was the same age and came from Retford. As well as Walter, in 1901 the family consisted of three daughters: Emily, (born 1887), Margaret (born 1889) and Edith (born 1891).

Although Walter was killed on the 9th August 1915 he was only reported missing and his mother and father were not informed of his death until December 1916, nearly sixteen months after Walter had been killed in action whilst serving in the Dardanelles. Walter, just twenty-three, was employed as a timber loader before he enlisted on 13 August 1914 with the 6th Lincs. This Battalion formed part of the 33rd Brigade, which in turn was a part of the 11th (Northern) Division. The Division was part of Kitchener's Army, coming into being on 21st August 1914. The Division was made up of volunteers and initially had very little equipment, including arms, with which to carry out their training at Belton, Grantham. However, the Division was deemed to be ready in May/June 1915 and was shipped off to Gallipoli from Liverpool via Alexandria and Mudros on 1st July 1915 on the Empress of Britain and the Aquitania. The Division took part in the Suvla Landings on 7th August 1915, and it must be assumed that Walter Holey was killed whilst taking part in the landings or the ensuing fighting.

Walter Holey has no known grave and is commemorated on the Helles Memorial, Gallipoli, Turkey.

PRIVATE HORACE DAVISON

593 Royal Army Medical Corps 2nd/1st East Lancs Field Ambulance.
Drowned 13th August 1915.

Horace Davison was one of eight children, and in 1901 all were living at 33 West Street, Retford. Horace's father, Charles (born 1860), was employed as a railway engineer; his mother Annie's (born 1862 in Lincoln) occupation is classed as undefined. The children in the family were Herbert (born 1882), employed as a fishmonger, Gertrude (born 1885), assistant to a dressmaker, Thomas (born 1888), classed as worker, Charles (born 1889), Fred (born 1891), Horace (born 1895), Florence (born 1897) and Walter (born 1899). In 1881 the family home had been 11 Chancery Lane, Retford, and the Census shows that Charles and Annie had a son Robert, aged one. Charles was then employed as an engine cleaner. By 1901 Robert was employed in Nottingham as a commercial clerk. He was a member of the East Retford Church Choir.

Horace attended Retford Grammar School and on leaving took up a post as teacher at the National School. With the outbreak of war Horace Davison enlisted in December 1914 becoming a private in the RAMC attached to the 2/1st East Lancs. Field Ambulance.

Horace died after the Royal Edward he was sailing on was sunk in the Aegean Sea after being struck from a torpedo fired from U-boat 14. As well as Horace, there were over a thousand other victims, including another Retford man, Frank Stockdale of 20 Richard Street, Retford. Both men had enlisted in Manchester in the 2/1st East Lancs. He was only twenty years old when he died.

The Royal Edward had sailed from Avonmouth on 28th/29th July 1915; having stopped at Malta and Alexandria on 10th August 1915, the ship left port on 12th August 1915 and was making its way to Mudros, one of the main island bases for the Gallipoli Campaign, when she was spotted by UB 14 at around 9 a.m. on 13th August, about 400 miles north of Alexandria. UB14 fired a torpedo, which hit the Royal Edward in the stern. The ship sank in less than ten minutes. Officers and troops from the Hampshires, Essex regiment South Wales Borders, Border Regiment King's Own Scottish Borderers, Army Service Corps, Royal Army Medical Corps, Lancashire Fusiliers and one member of the Royal Engineers all perished. One of the officers to die was Temporary Major Cuthbert Bromley, Lancashire Fusiliers, one of the famous "Six VCs Before Breakfast".

Horace's death was reported in the Retford Times on 3rd September 1915. The report stated that "Deep sympathy is felt for Mr. and Mrs. Davison of Albert Road, Retford, whose son Private Horace Davison 2/1 Lancs. Field Ambulance is reported by the War Office as "missing feared drowned" as a consequence of the loss of the Royal Edward on 13th August 1915.

A letter of sympathy has been received from the officers and it is also signed by a surviving colleague. It runs "We have received a letter from Lieut. Cockcroft, the surviving officer of the men on board the Royal Edward. He enclosed a list of those who were saved and we are sincerely sorry that your son is missing. We feel that we would like to offer you our sincere heartfelt sympathy. It has always been the boast of the Ambulance that the members were united, not merely by association but by firmer bonds: of comradeship and true friendship. We, who had the privilege of knowing and appreciating Pte Davison, feel that his death would leave a gap, which we could never fill. The consolation remains that such a death at the post of duty is the highest sacrifice of a true patriot".   ,

The "Royal Edward"
Entering Avonmouth Dock.

Mr. E Lidster, headmaster of the National School, where the deceased was formerly a teacher, wrote the following letter to Mr. and Mrs. Davison: "I am grieved to hear the news of your bereavement. I can hardly realise that poor Horace will not return amongst us, for I have looked forward to his coming back to help me. Another bright young life scarified in this awful war. Few indeed will be the homes where sorrow will not be found. You have the sincere sympathy of myself and staff and we trust that you will find comfort in the fact that the boy was a thorough English lad and that he nobly answered the Call of Duty. I little thought a few weeks ago that was to be our last meeting".

Horace has no known grave and is commemorated on the Helles Memorial, Gallipoli, Turkey.

PRIVATE FRANK STOCKDALE
460 Royal Army Medical Corps 2nd/1st East Lancs Field Ambulance.
Drowned 13th August 1915.

Frank Stockdale, the son of Charles and Charity Stockdale, who resided at 20 (Kendle Cottage) Richard Street, was another victim of the sinking of the Royal Edward. He and Horace Davison had joined the East Lancs. RAMC at the same time in Manchester. Along with Sgt Arthur Phillipson, Pte. Ernest King and Lance Corporal Scott, Frank was a regular worshipper at St Alban's Church.

Frank enlisted in November 1914. Previously, he was in the employ of Messrs W J Jenkins and Co as an apprentice fitter. He was aged just nineteen years when he died. As well as Frank, Mr and Mrs Stockdale had two other sons who served in the war: Lance Corp. J W Stockdale of the 3/2nd East Lancs. Field Ambulance, Sapper Joseph Stockdale in the Doncaster Company.

Frank has no known grave and is commemorated on the Helles Memorial, Gallipoli, Turkey.

CAPTAIN WILLIAM EYRE

12th Battalion Welch Regiment (attached to the 1st Battalion Lancashire Fusiliers). Died 19th August 1915.

Captain William Eyre was the only son of William and Mary Eyre, who resided at 21 Babworth Road, Retford. William Snr was a retired miller at the time of the outbreak of the war and originally came from Derbyshire. Mary Eyre came originally from Morton, near Gainsborough. William Jnr. was born at Creswell on March 25th 1879. Educated at Retford Grammar School, he went on to Sheffield University and London University where he gained an Honours degree in Chemistry.

Following this success William returned to be a Master at Retford Grammar School. He remained at the school for a number of years as a science teacher, before he moved to Cranbrook School in Kent. In 1907 he joined the staff at Christ's Hospital, Horsham, as science master and housemaster. He volunteered on the outbreak of war and was gazetted into the 8th Service of the Welch Regiment as a Captain. He was at a later date transferred to the 12th Battalion, and subsequently he was attached to the1st Lancashire Fusiliers.

It was with the Fusiliers that he went to the Dardanelles on 15th July 1915 and was wounded during action near Gully Beach on 6th August 1915. He was removed to the 19th General Hospital at Alexandria, Egypt, where he succumbed to his injuries on 19th August 1915.

He was commemorated on a memorial stone at Retford Grammar School, which was placed in the Fives Court.

William Eyre is buried at the Alexandria (Chatby) Military and War Memorial Cemetery in Egypt.

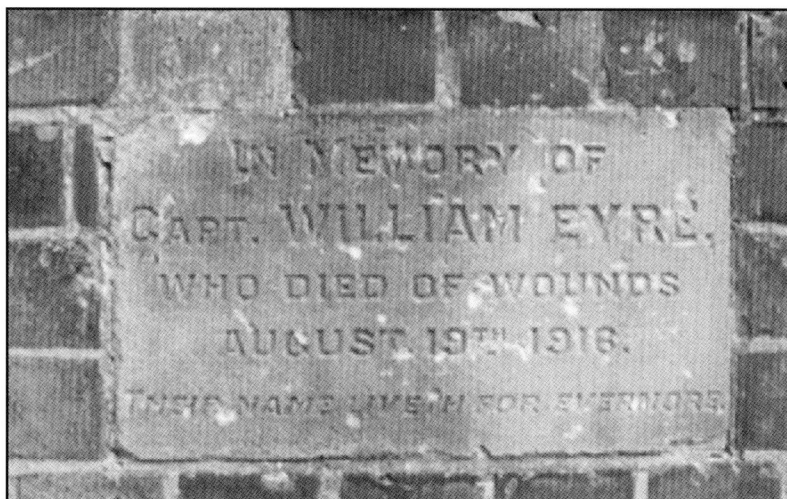

SERGEANT EDWARD CASBURNE
13054 9th Sherwood Foresters (Notts and Derby Regiment) 'D' Company
Killed 27th August 1915.

The 1891 Census shows Edward Casburne to be two months old, living in Oulton with Woodlesford (which can be found five miles southeast of Leeds) with his parents, Frederick W and Anne Elizabeth. The 1901 Census has Edward, aged ten, still living in the same place with his parents; his father was employed as a bricklayer's labourer. By this time there was an addition to the family – Mabel. At some point the family, or at least Edward, moved to the Retford area, and was living at Hayton near Retford when he enlisted in the army. He was killed in action on 27th August 1915.

Edward has no known grave and is commemorated on the Helles Memorial, Gallipoli, Turkey.

PRIVATE WALTER (TINY) DAVISON
14390 10th Battalion Sherwood Foresters (Notts and Derby Regiment).
Died 28th August 1915.

Walter Davison's mother, who lived at Rectory Road, received the sad information of the death of her son a year to the day after the he had enlisted. The Rev. Buchanan, C of E Chaplain at the No 10 Clearing Station (Lijssenthoek, Belgium), where Walter died, wrote: "I am very sorry to have to tell you that your son Private Davison of the 10th Sherwood Foresters was brought into the hospital last night very severely wounded in the head and died shortly after. I saw him before he died and said a prayer for him but he was quite unconscious."

Captain J W Fisher says, "I very much regret that it is my duty to tell you that your son Private (W) Davison was wounded in the trenches on 27th and has died of wounds. At the time he was tending to another wounded man. I must express how sorry I am to have lost him. He always did his work well."

Pte Davison, had been a stretcher-bearer and had been in France about eight weeks and in the trenches nearly a fortnight when he was killed.

Walter was formerly employed at the station as a railway porter, and was at the time the second Retford railway man to be killed, the other being Herbert Grant of the 8th Sherwood Foresters. He was 24 years of age.

In his last letter home Pte Davison said, "I am writing from the trenches this time. We are having a rough time of it. We are not in the fire trenches but the reserves. There is a Chateau, just like an Old English Hall against us and the Germans dropped about twenty shells on us yesterday, only about 30 to 50 yards away from our dug-out. They blow bricks and dirt about 40 feet into the air. Bullets are always flying about; we cannot see them coming, only hear them whizz past our ear. We have not had many hurt, only one poor lad killed yesterday. I had to carry him out. It is the snipers who do all the damage. It is very hard work carrying the wounded out of the trenches. We have to be very careful and it does half make us sweat and blow. I got a shirt and two pairs of socks from Mrs Bradshaw the day previous to coming here".

Walter Davison is buried in Lijssenthoek Cemetery, Belgium.

PRIVATE ARTHUR CLARK CHANDLER
13626 2nd Battalion Sherwood Foresters(Notts and Derby Regiment).
Died 7th September 1915.

Pte Arthur C Chandler was the fifth son of Mr and Mrs Chandler of 56 Nelson Street, and was part of a large family of ten children: six boys and four girls. As well as Arthur, there were three other brothers who served: Walter, 8th Sherwoods; Albert, Royal Engineers; and Leonard, also of 8th Sherwoods (Leonard, the youngest son, was to die on 15th April 1916). Arthur, like all his brothers, attended Thrumpton School when Mr L Clements was headteacher and all were choir- boys at St. Alban's Church.

Their father had previously been a soldier with the Sherwood Foresters and had served in the Boer War; at the time of Arthur's death he was in the employ of Messrs. Jenkins and Son.

Arthur, prior to joining up in January 1915 for the duration, was employed by the Great Northern Railway as a signalman in the northern box at Retford Station. Previously he had been employed by Walter Yoell, jeweller and watchmaker of Carolgate, Retford, with his brother Leonard.

Arthur died of wounds at the 10th Casualty Clearing Station, St Omer, and is buried at Longuenesse (St Omer) Souvenir Cemetery, France.

Pte Chandler received his wounds during the major action at Hooge on 9th August 1915 and died five weeks later, on 7th September. His mother was first notified on 12th August, when she received a telegram saying that he had been dangerously wounded. A letter sent from Sister V. Rogers a week before Arthur's death states that "Your son Arthur is not quite so well today. For the last few days he has been brighter, and though he could not talk much has quite understood what has been said to him.

Your letters and several others which have lately come for him he quite understood and appreciated. He knew all the different names quite well, and even when I asked him what I should say to his mother he said give her my love. Today he is quite unable to speak and I think he has not understood much. He looks tired and weary though not, I think, suffering much. I am afraid the end is not far away. He has been very good and patient. With kind regards, yours sincerely, V Rogers, Sister."

Before his death Arthur received a visit from his brother Leonard.

LIEUTENANT WALTER EDWIN STOCKDALE
Nottinghamshire Sherwood Rangers Yeomanry.
Killed 10th September 1915.

"Lieutenant Walter Stockdale was a well-known cricketer and hockey-player in the Retford district" (Wisden Almanac Obituaries 1915). He was the son of Richard Hugh Stockdale of Allison House, Sutton, near Retford.

Walter was killed in action in the Dardanelles and is buried in Green Hill Cemetery, Gallipoli, Turkey.

Below is a photograph of Squadron Sergeant Major Walter Edwin Stockdale on camp in Babworth Park, near Retford. The photograph was taken in 1912 and shows Walter wearing khaki battle-dress.

RIFLEMAN ALFRED REGISTER
S/3527 12th Battalion The Rifle Brigade.
Killed 25th September 1915.

Alfred was born in Pyebank, Yorkshire in 1891. His father, Thomas, lived on Leverton Road, Retford.

Alfred has no known grave and is commemorated on the Ploegsteert Memorial, Belgium.

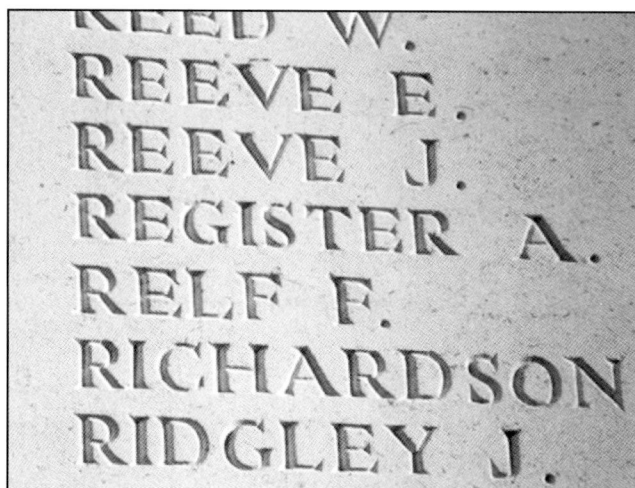

PRIVATE WILLIAM BREDDY
23267 10th Battalion York and Lancaster Regiment.
Killed 26th September 1915.

In the 1911 Census William was living with his wife, Florrie, at his mother's house at 21 Spital Hill, along with four of his younger siblings. He was employed as a jobbing iron foundry worker. Florrie remarried in 1917.

William Breddy has no known grave and is commemorated on the Loos Memorial, France.

PRIVATE GEORGE MERRILLS
28429 2nd Battalion Cheshire Regiment.
Died 3rd October 1915.

Son of Annie and George Merrills, Pte George Merrills resided at 12 Woolpack Street, Retford. He was only eighteen years old when he was killed in action in and around the Hohenzollern Redoubt on 3rd October 1915.

George Merrills has no known grave and is commemorated on the Loos Memorial, France.

PRIVATE ALBERT SUTTON
15029 2nd Battalion Sherwood Foresters (Notts and Derby Regiment).
Killed 5th October 1915.

Mr and Mrs Sutton, whilst living at of 1 Ridgeway Buildings, West Street, received the sad news that their son, Pte Albert Sutton of the 2nd Sherwood Foresters, had been killed in action in Belgium on 5th October. He was twenty-three, and had been employed on the Great Central Railway as a painter. In a letter he wrote to his parents just before going to the front he said," I am going to fight for a living. I've got to do my bit along with anyone else. Don't let it bother you. I am all right and I shall expect to be back in Retford some time. We have just got to keep the flag flying." His younger brother Walter, aged eighteen, saw action as a gunner in the Royal Field Artillery in the Dardanelles.

Albert Sutton is buried in Potijze Burial Ground Cemetery, Belgium.

LANCE CORPORAL CLARENCE HOLLIDAY
13558 9th Battalion Sherwood Foresters (Notts and Derby Regiment).
Killed 6th October 1915.

Retford Times 29th October 1915

ORDSALL SOLDIER KILLED
"News has been received that Corporal Clarence Holliday of the Sherwood Foresters, second son of F Holliday of 6a Church Lane, Ordsall, died of wounds on 6th October whilst serving in the Dardanelles. The brave soldier, who was only twenty-two, was formerly employed on the Great Northern Railway and enlisted very shortly after the outbreak of the hostilities. He was wounded some time ago in France and after his recovery was sent to the Dardanelles.

Much sympathy is felt with Mr Holliday in the loss of his son, who was highly respected in a wide circle of friends. Mr Holliday has been employed at the Northern Rubber Works for twenty-six years."

Clarence Holliday has no known grave and is commemorated on the Helles Memorial, Gallipoli, Turkey.

PRIVATE LEONARD TOMLINSON
2619 2nd Battalion York and Lancashire Regiment, 'C' Company.
Killed 29th October 1915.

Pte Leonard Tomlinson was the son of John and Emma Tomlinson, 57 Spital Hill, Retford, and the brother of George Tomlinson, who had died earlier in the war. He had been in France for about twelve months when he was killed, and had forfeited a promotion to Lance Corporal in order to find his brother's grave. (George is commemorated on the Menin Gate in Ypres).

A letter received from Pte M Murry said, "I write these few lines on behalf of No. 3 Section to which your son belonged and I am very sorry to tell you that he was killed on 29th October. He died a hero's death. He was carrying messages. Leonard and I were great friends and I am sure he was everybody's chum.

When I came out in February he was the only one I knew… I am sorry you have lost both your sons in this terrible war." A further letter was received from Second Lieutenant H L Ward saying, "It is with deep regret that I have to inform you of the death of your son Leonard. He was killed in the execution of his duty during a bombardment and it might be some consolation to know that death was instantaneous. He was the runner of my platoon and this is a post of responsibility only given to the best man…. You may rest assured that he died a death that any mother might be proud of, carrying on his duties with death all around him and, when his time came, dying that England might live."

Leonard Tomlinson is buried at Potijze Burial Ground Cemetery, Belgium.

*Leonard Tomlinson's gravestone
at Potijze Burial Ground*

PRIVATE FRANK FARRAND
1474 1st/8th Sherwood Foresters (Notts and Derby Regiment).
Killed 14th October 1915.

Reported in Retford Times of 1916: Death of Frank Farrand on 14th October 1915

"The picture shown is a reproduction of a photograph of the late Pte Frank Farrand, of the 1/8th

Notts and Derbys regiment, second son of Mr and Mrs Frank Farrand, 36 West Street, Retford. The deceased, who was in his twentieth year when he was killed, had been in the Territorials for over four years, and before the war was employed in the GNR cleaning sheds in Retford. Six months ago the parents received information that their son had been reported as missing and on Sunday last, the sad news was received from the Lichfield Record Office that Frank was killed in action on 14 October 1915."

Frank Farrand has no known grave and is commemorated on the Loos Memorial, France.

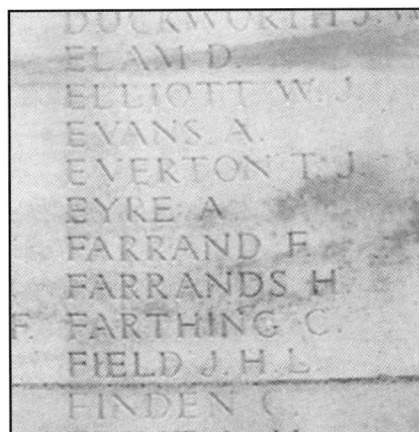

CORPORAL JOHN WILLIAM DARWIN
9904 The Border Regiment.
Died 8th October 1915.

A report in the Retford Times a week before his death stated that Corporal Darwin, son of John William and Bridget Amelia Darwin was in St George's Hospital, Malta, with dysentery. He unfortunately succumbed to the disease and died at the age of 24 and is buried in Addolorata Cemetery, Malta. John was born in Govan, Lanarkshire, but his soldier father, also called John, had returned to his birthplace in Retford when he retired.

Edgar who was killed on the morning of 27th October (1915). He was shot in the head and death was instantaneous. Sid Colton, Edgar and I were so happy the few minutes we were together one night last week. Edgar was the only pal I had in the Battalion, so you will guess how I miss him. He was well liked by everybody."

The report included another letter, written by the Reverend Churchward, Chaplain to the Forces, reaffirming that Edgar had been shot in the head by a sniper and that he was buried in a little cemetery behind the lines near a place called Laventie. He also pointed out that the grave would be cared for and that a cross had been erected by the Battalion. Edgar White was twenty-four years of age

Edgar White is buried at the Royal Irish Rifles Graveyard, Laventie, France.

PRIVATE NOEL BUTTON
13021 D Company 9th Battalion Sherwood Foresters (Notts and Derby Regiment).
Killed 1st November 1915.

Pte Button, whose parents lived at 10 Myrtle Street, is buried in the same cemetery as Joseph Johnson having belonged to the same Battalion. He died whilst serving during the Gallipoli Campaign.

Noel Button is buried at Hill 10 Cemetery, Gallipoli, Turkey.

CORPORAL VINCENT PATTERSON
9339 3rd Battalion Lincolnshire Regiment.
Died 7th November 1915.

Cpl Vincent Patterson's death was reported in the Retford Times in November under the headline, "A Soldier Family", in which the efforts of the family in the war are described.

Unfortunately Vincent's surname is spelt Pattison in the report, though all records show his name to be spelt Patterson, including his gravestone in Retford Cemetery.

The report shows photographs of Corporal Vincent in his Boer War uniform as well as pictures of his soldier sons, Alfred and Kimberley (see below). Alfred died at the age of seventeen on 16th June

1915 whilst serving with the 1st Lincolnshires. Kimberley was reclaimed from the army on account of his age; he was only fifteen and had served fourteen months with 9th East Yorks. Vincent Pattison had served in the South African War, which possibly explains Kimberley's name, and had been a regular soldier for twenty-eight years; at the outbreak of war he volunteered his services again. Although an old Retford reservist, he and his family were residing at 22 Abney Street, Sheffield at the time of his death.

Alfred Patterson aged seventeen, Vincent Patterson aged forty-three and Kimberley Patterson aged fifteen.

PRIVATE JOSEPH JOHNSON
13507 9th Battalion Sherwood Foresters.
Died 14th November 1915.

Pte Joseph Johnson originated from Manchester, where his father, William, in 1901 was a labourer in a cotton mill. In 1901 he lived at 67, Gleden Street, Manchester with his father William, mother Mary, sisters Beatrice, Mary, and Gertrude, and a younger brother, William, as well as a lodger, Mary Barratt, and his grandmother Susannah. He moved to Retford around 1912 to live with his sister, Mrs G B Darwin, who was the daughter-in-law of the well-known Newsagents on Carolgate Bridge, G B Darwin. Before joining up on 23rd August 1914, Joseph was employed at Wm Jenkins. He was twenty-three when he

was killed during the Gallipoli Campaign towards the end of this disastrous campaign on 14th November 1915. The Battalion were in the front line on 11th November behind Jephson's Post.

Joseph would have been involved in a number of engagements, in particular the Suvla Landings in August 1915.

Joseph Johnson is buried in Hill 10 Cemetery, Gallipoli, Turkey.

PRIVATE JOHN WILLIAM ANDERSON
11447 7th Battalion Leicestershire Regiment
Died on 27th November 1915.

John Anderson was born in Bawtry in 1885; by 1901 he was living in Retford and employed as a draper's assistant. He had a change in career and was working for the Corporation as a labourer when he enlisted with the colours in September 1914. By this time he was also married and living at 6 St John Street, Retford. So it was his wife who received the sad news that he had been killed in action leaving her with three children under 10 years of age. He had been in France for five months.

2nd Lieutenant Edward Kingsley Wakeford (himself to be killed as a Lieutenant, aged only twenty-two, during the Battle of the Somme on 16th July 1916) wrote to John's wife, saying, " I am writing to let you know that your husband was killed today whilst on sentry duty. Death was instantaneous. I know nothing I can say can do much to lessen your sorrow but I should like you to know that he had the goodwill and the respect of us all. And that we all offer you our deepest sympathy."

John Anderson is buried in Bienvillers Military Cemetery, France.

PRIVATE CHARLES HENRY GRANT
13506 9th Battalion Sherwood Foresters (Notts and Derby Regiment).
Killed 27th November 1915.

Pte Charles Grant was one of the first to volunteer in Retford. Following his training at Belton, near Grantham, he went overseas to the Dardanelles on 1st July 1915. Before his enlistment he was employed as a painter and decorator with Messr G Huskinson, who was based in the Market Square. Charles was born in Johannesburg, South Africa. His father, J H Grant, died in Cape Town in 1901. Charles, whose mother worked as housekeeper at West Retford Hall, was a worshipper at West Retford Church.

Charles Grant has no known grave and is commemorated on the Helles Memorial, Gallipoli.

PRIVATE ABRAHAM HEATH
15127 10th Battalion Sherwood Foresters (Notts and Derby Regiment).
Died on 12th December 1915.

Abraham Heath was thirty-five years of age when he died of wounds received in action. A letter Mrs Heath received at their home, 85 Albert Road, stated that Abraham had been badly wounded in the right thigh and that he succumbed to his injuries in a hospital in Boulogne. Before his enlistment he had worked at Bradshaw's Foundry for twenty years. It would appear that this was a family tradition as his father and a brother, Thomas, also worked at the Foundry. Another brother, John Heath Jnr, worked at Ordsall Iron Works.

Abraham Heath is buried in Boulogne Eastern Cemetery, France.

1916

PRIVATE GEORGE WHITLAM
10604 Lincolnshire Regiment
Died 13th January 1916

"Amidst many manifestations of deep sympathy and respect for one of Retford's gallant sons, the remains were laid to rest in the cemetery on Monday of Pte George Whitlam, 1st Lincoln Regiment. The deceased was the third son of Mrs Whitlam and the late Mr John Whitlam of 81 Whinney Moore Lane, Thrumpton. The brave lad, who was formerly employed by Mr David Benson, West Retford, enlisted on August 17th 1914. He was deeply moved by pictures of the German atrocities, which appeared in the papers at the time and remarked that he could not stay at home while such things were occurring in Belgium. He was at Neuve Chapelle, Hill 60, and Loos and experienced several narrow escapes. On one occasion his rifle was blown out of his hands by a shell and his only means of defence was a knife. In November he received a gunshot wound in the foot and died in Boscombe Hospital from the effects of the wound". Retford Times

Private Whitlam, who was twenty-five, was given a military funeral. The band of the 1/4th East Yorkshire Regiment played Chopin's Funeral March and The Dead March in Saul on the way to the cemetery. The coffin, which was draped with the Union Jack, was borne on a gun carriage provided by the Durham RFA, and the buglers of the Durham Light Infantry sounded the Last Post over the grave. The service, which was conducted by the Rev Paxton, Vicar of St Saviour's, was very impressive.

The chief mourners were Mrs Whitlam, (mother), Ptes. T Whitlam, C Whitlam, and H Whitlam and Master E Whitlam (brothers), Mr and Mrs Saul (brother-in-law and sister), Mr and Mrs Downer (brother-in-law and sister), the Misses Maggie and Lily Whitlam (sisters), Mrs Shirdon (aunt), and Mr and Mrs Howitt (uncle and aunt), and Mr Simpson (brother-in-law).

Mrs Whitlam had three other sons serving King and Country. One was Pte G Whitlam, 6th Lincs, who was wounded on 9th August 1915 at Suvla. The eldest, Pte.Thomas Whitlam of the 2nd York and Lancaster Regiment, had been at the front seven months when he was wounded in the left arm. The youngest, Trooper H Whitlam of the Sherwood Rangers Yeomanry, contracted an illness in Cairo and was sent home. H Whitlam had sold a hairdressing business at Askern (near Doncaster) to enlist. Mrs Whitlam was a widow and much sympathy was shown to her and the "patriotic family".

George Whitlam is buried in East Retford Cemetery.

PRIVATE HERBERT COOLING
11456 1st Battlion Grenadier Guards.
Killed 24th January 1916.

Pte Herbert Cooling was killed whilst on sentry duty with the Battalion on 26th January 1916. Herbert had been a regular soldier and was called up on the outbreak of hostilities. He was the son of Sarah Ann and Robert Cooling, who resided in Bolham Lane, Retford. Robert, who was deceased at the time of Herbert's death, had been a maltster's labourer and was born in Newark. Sarah Ann came from Misterton. In 1881 they had four daughters and a son (Mary, Alice, George, Anne and Sarah). Herbert was born in 1886.

Prior to being called up Herbert worked at Waleswood Colliery. After being called up, he spent the first three months of the war carrying out specialist police duties in London. He was sent to France in November 1914 and went through some very hard and bitter fighting. He was in fact wounded on three occasions.

In February 1915 a letter from H Cooling, Grenadier Guards, was published in the Retford Times:
'We have had some awful weather, rain and snow. I have had frost in my feet. I think that will get better as the weather improves. We don't mind the fighting so much. The Germans will get smashed up as the weather gets better and don't forget it! We have held them all winter and stuck at it like Britons. We have had plenty to eat. The people of England have looked after us. We have four days in the trenches and four days out. We sleep in barns or anywhere we can get on straw. You want to see the farms and villages all blown up; cows pigs, horse and things are laid in all directions…
I shall be glad when it is all over. You will see a great difference shortly as the weather gets better and we advance all along the line. Thanks for the parcel: I shall be glad of anything you send."

On 12th January 1916 the 1st Battalion Grenadier Guards had moved to Laventie and from there went into the trenches at Picantin, every alternate forty-eight hours taking turns with the 4th Battalion and the 2nd Irish Guards. Herbert was shot whilst on sentry duty.

A letter received by Mrs Sarah Cooling from a fellow soldier, Pte Smith, said, "It is with regret I write to tell you of your son's death. It was great shock to me, as I had been having a bit of a talk to him in the morning and at night I heard he had been killed. He is buried as nicely as we could. The chaplain read the service and a cross marks his grave in the little cemetery at …………. I will tell you the name some time as we are not allowed to mention it now."

Herbert Cooling is buried in the Rue-de-Bacquerot (13th London) Graveyard, Laventie, France.

LANCE SERGEANT WILLIAM HAROLD LEE
18137 6th Battalion King's Own Yorkshire Light Infantry.
Died 26th January 1916

Sergeant W H Lee: Brave Retford Soldier Killed
Retford Times January 1916
"The life of another young Retfordian has been sacrificed in the fight for right and justice against might. He is Sergeant W H Lee, 6th KOYLI, the third son of Mr and Mrs W Lee, 20 Cross Street, Newtown, Retford. The gallant lad met with his death on January 26th whilst conducting his men to a place of safety, a shell bursting near the parapet killing him and another young fellow."

The above is how the Retford Times reported the death of William Harold Lee, aged just twenty-one. William, or Harold as he liked to be known, attended the Thrumpton Council School, and on leaving gained a job as a messenger boy with the Post Office. Having gained promotion he worked in Doncaster as a postman, and was one of the first to enlist from his work, on 27th August 1914. He went to France on 21st May 1915 and was promoted to Sergeant just before entering the trenches. He was involved in action at Loos, Hooge and in and around Ypres. Just before Christmas 1914, Pte Lee, as he then was, had a chance of coming home on leave but actually forfeited the right so a fellow soldier whose mother was dangerously ill could have leave.

In a letter home his 2nd Lieutenant wrote, "I regret to have to inform you that your son, Sgt Lee No 18137, was killed in the trenches. The enemy's shell burst just in front of the trench, blowing the parapet down, causing the death of your son and another. His body was carried down to Battalion Headquarters, which is about a mile behind the line, and there the funeral service was observed. The news of your son's death was received by those who knew him with much regret and sorrow. He was a general favourite among us, the men doing anything he told them to with goodwill, and you can be sure he can ill be spared. He was always cheerful under the most trying conditions. Do not grieve for him too much, but rather take most pride in believing that he was a worthy son and that he had taken not an insignificant part in exterminating Prussian Militarism."

Pte Sam Vallance, who, it was said, was the only Retford lad left in the Battalion, wrote: "Poor Harold, my best chum, has been killed in fighting for his King and Country. There is one consolation, that Harold died a hero and had a peaceful death. I am heartbroken. He was very popular with his comrades and was very well respected and liked".

William Lee is buried in New Irish Farm Cemetery, Belgium.

PRIVATE ROBERT JAMES DRAKEFIELD

21699 10th Battalion Sherwood Foresters (Notts and Derby Regiment).
Killed 14th February 1916.

Robert Drakefield was the son of George and Elizabeth Ann Drakefield. The family lived at 21 Station Road, Retford in 1901. Elizabeth, born in 1859, came from Ashby de la Zouch whilst George, also born in 1859, originated from Derbyshire and was employed as a railway engine driver.

Robert Drakefield was one of three men named on the Retford memorial who died during the same action on 13/14th February 1916, the others being Sam Cook and Walter Rogan (see below), defending what was known as the Bluff (an accumulation of spoil formed with the building of the Ypres-Comines Canal, the steeper slopes facing the enemy, with the British ensconced on the top of the ridge.

It was during this stint in the trenches that steel helmets were worn for the first time by the 10th Battalion. On relieving the 7th Lincolnshires on the night of 13/14th February, all seemed to go well, but the next twenty-four hours, according to The History of the 10th Battalion during the Great War (Lieut W N Hoyte), "tested the fighting qualities of the battalion severely."

At about 8.30 am on 14th February it would appear that the German artillery, including trench mortars and rifle grenades, spent time registering (a process of getting the range of the targets to be attacked). This went on for approximately two hours, only to be followed by a bombardment of great intensity at 2.30 pm. At 5.40 p.m. a mine was exploded under the trenches, particularly those occupied by 'C' Company.

There followed immediately an attack by the German infantry, some of whom reached the top of the Bluff, only to be driven off. The loss of the Bluff would have been a severe blow to the British and such was the threat that the 7th Btn Border Regiment and two companies of the 7th Btn Lincolnshire Regiment were used to reinforce the line, and a possible counter-attack was considered.

The 10th Btn Sherwood Foresters were eventually relieved; but by this time heavy losses had been inflicted (16 Officers and 344 other ranks killed, wounded or missing).

Robert Drakefield has no known grave and is commemorated on the Menin Gate Memorial, Begium.

LANCE SERGEANT WALTER ROGAN

15128 10th Battalion Sherwood Foresters (Notts and Derby Regiment).
Killed 14th February 1916.

Mrs Rogan, 39 Beardsall Row, Retford, received a letter of sympathy from the Rev. J Thwaites Mumford who had been vicar of East Retford and was serving as chaplain at Alexandria, in reference to the death of her husband, Lance Sergeant Walter Hogan, who was killed in February 1916 in France. Walter Rogan had been only five weeks abroad. Mrs Rogan was left with five young children and her husband had not seen the baby. In the course of his letter Rev Mumford wrote: "This will cause a great blank in your life, but you will feel proud of being the wife of one who gave his life for his country".

Walter Rogan is buried in Spoilbank Cemetery, Belgium.

PRIVATE SAMUEL COOK

21442 10th Battalion Sherwood Foresters (Notts and Derby Regiment).
Killed 14th February 1916.

Below is a report taken from the Retford Times.

Samuel Cook, Sherwood Foresters, son of Mr and Mrs Cook, Little Lane, Moorgate, Retford, had been posted missing by the War Office in February 1916. The receipt of the following letter from the Enquiry Department of the Red Cross and Order of St John, however, gave little hope to the family of his safety: "Since you enquired at our office for your missing son, I regret to say a very sad report has reached us concerning him. It comes from Pte G Briggs in hospital abroad, place unknown, who states that your son and four other men were all in front line trench at the Bluff, St Eloi, he himself being in the support trench just behind. He saw the front trench blown up by a mine and thinks that all men were instantly killed, that is to say, buried by the explosion. It was impossible to recover their bodies afterwards, and this accounts for the War Office posting your son as missing. I am afraid after this distinct account we are not likely to hear any better news about your son, but if we do we will at once write to you again. Please believe how sorry we are to send you these sad tidings".

Pte Cook joined the Foresters in December 1914 and left for France on 15 December 1915. He was twenty-two, and was previously employed at the Northern Rubber Works. Two other brothers served: George Cook, Sherwood Foresters (T.F) in France, and Alfred Cook, 2/8 Sherwood Foresters in Ireland.

Samuel Cook has no known grave and is commemorated on the Menin Gate Memorial, Belgium.

PRIVATE LEWIS THOMPSON DAVISON
590 10th Battalion Lincolnshire Regiment (Grimsby Chums).
Died on 26th February 1916.

News was been received in Retford of the death of another of "Retford's gallant sons on the field of Battle" (Retford Times). Pte Thompson was thirty-nine when he met his death in France on 26th February 1916. The Battalion arrived in France on 10th January 1916 having undergone a period of training since its formation. More training followed in France and finally the Battalion moved up to the front lines on 24th February.

Two days later Pte Thompson was killed, being amongst the first of the "Chums" to die on duty in France. He was the son of John Davison, who had been a butcher on Carolgate. Pte Thompson, prior to enlisting, was employed at Messrs Clark and Co, Laundry.

In a change of jobs he moved Grimsby to work on the docks and it was here that he enlisted, joining the "Grimsby Chums", a pals' battalion.

Lewis Davison is buried in Brewery Orchard Cemetery, Bois-Grenier, France.

PRIVATE THOMAS J SMITH
15570 7th Battalion Northamptonshire Regiment,
Killed 11th March 1916.

Pte T J Smith of the Northants Regiment was killed on 11th March 1916. His father, Mr Joseph Smith, lived at Manor Cottages, Ordsall, Retford at the time of his son's death He had been in the war theatre since September 1915. Before joining up, Thomas had been an apprentice for five years to Messrs Loseby and Son, the Retford Tailors and Outfitters. At some stage he went to work for Messrs Webb Bros in Market Harborough. He was twenty-one when he was killed and had been in the Army since

1914. Joseph Smith had been a farmer at Littleborough and had two sons at the time of T J Smith's death: J E G Smith, a grocer and provisions dealer, and H Smith, a farmer at Drakeholes, Wiseton, near Retford.

Thomas Smith is buried in Menin Road South Military Cemetery, Belgium.

PRIVATE LEONARD CHANDLER
1865 Sherwood Foresters (Notts and Derby Regiment).
Died 15th April 1916.

In an issue of the Retford Times it was recorded that Pte Leonard Chandler, the youngest son of Mr and Mrs Chandler, 56 Nelson Street Retford had been wounded in the thigh by shrapnel. Within a short time, the Times reported that it is "our painful duty to announce the death of the gallant boy, who died on Saturday last as a result of the wounds. Mr and Mrs Chandler's grief is all the more poignant because of the fact that Leonard wrote home a very bright and cheery letter on the 13th in which he stated he was "getting on alright and expected to be in England shortly". Chaplain G H Donald also wrote the following: "I was visiting some of our boys in hospital today and spoke to your son. He is getting on very well. He is quite cheerful and looks well, although he suffers a good deal of pain when his wounds are being dressed. He will probably be sent down to a hospital at Base and will write to you from there. He is having every care and attention and the best of skill. He's a fine fellow."

Apparently Pte Chandler suffered a relapse and the sad information of his death was conveyed in the following letter from Chaplain H A Forbes: "I regret to have to inform you that your son, Pte L Chandler, Sherwood Foresters (TF), died of wounds here on the 15th inst. and is buried in the cemetery here. As I have just arrived, I am sorry I cannot give you any particulars. With sincere sympathy with you in your great sorrow".

This was the second son of Mr and Mrs Chandler to make the great sacrifice for King and Country, Pte Arthur Clarke Chandler dying in 1915 as a result of wounds.

Two other sons and a son-in-law also served with the Colours: Pte Walter Chandler, the eldest, was a Territorial; Sapper Albert Chandler joined the Royal Engineers, while the son-in-law, Pte A Millington, was is in the Sherwood Foresters. The father served with the Sherwood Foresters through the South African Campaign and was an employee at Messrs W J Jenkins and Co., Engineering Works.

Leonard Chandler is buried in the Aubigny Communal Cemetery Extension, France.

SERGEANT WILLIAM HILEY MARKHAM

60 8th Battalion Sherwood Foresters (Notts and Derby Regiment).
Killed 17th April 1916.

The Retford Times reported: "It is our painful duty to report the death of another brave Territorial - Sergeant W. Markham, Sherwood Foresters, the eldest son of Band Sergeant and Mrs Markham of Moorgate. The news of the young hero's death was sent by Sergeant Bescoby, who wrote: 'A mine had been sprung and the crater had to be taken and consolidated. It was during this action that Will was struck on the head. I do not know exactly what kind of missile it was; but be assured of this: he died instantaneously and suffered no pain. He will be buried alongside so many other brave soldiers who have laid down their lives for the cause for which we are fighting. It was a terrible blow for my section of the old Band and for all the Retfordians in the Regiment. Please accept the sincere sympathy of all in your great sorrow."

The deceased was very popular and highly esteemed by his many friends. He was formerly employed by the Northern Rubber Company. He was a clever wrestler and weightlifter and had won wrestling competitions".

The Battalion History states that the Battalion went back into the Vimy Ridge Sector on 12th April 1916 for an eight-day stretch. The trenches were in a poor state because of the snow and rain. The time they spent in the trenches on this tour were described as the most "eventful" whilst in that sector.

On 16th April 1916, the French were to explode a mine (that to which Sergeant Bescoby alludes above), which was to be followed up by a raiding party. Whilst trying to consolidate positions around the crater lip following the explosion, Sergeant Markham was killed "gallantly controlling the fire of his platoon for nearly two hours under very heavy fire".

Sgt Markham, according to The Battalion History, was shot through the head and died instantly.

William Markham is buried in Ecoivres Military Cemetery, Mont-St Eloi, France.

YEOMAN OF SIGNALS GEORGE LISTER
227230 Royal Navy.
Killed 31st May 1916.

George Lister was killed in HMS Chester in the Jutland battle of 31st May 1916. He was First Class Petty Officer. He was stationed on the bridge doing his duty as a signaller. Shortly after the ship came under fire, a shell passed right across the bridge and burst close by where he was standing. A fragment of the shell struck him on the head and death was instantaneous.

On the morning after the action, the Captain read the burial service over all the gallant dead, and they were buried at sea with full military honours. His Commanding Officer spoke of him as not only a highly trained Yeoman Signalman, but also as a splendid example of a gallant British sailor.

George Lister is commemorated on the Chatham Naval Memorial.

LANCE CORPORAL FRANK BENNETT MM
432352 Canadian Infantry.
Died 2nd June 1916.

Frank Bennett was born on 3rd July 1890 in Chesterfield, Derbyshire. At some stage in his life Frank must have emigrated to Canada, where he took up employment as a gardener, possibly in Edmonton, Alberta, as this is where he attested to join the army. Frank enlisted on 6th January 1915 and was placed with the 49th Battalion of the Alberta Regiment (Canadian Infantry).

He was the son of Samuel and Mary E Bennett, who at the time of his death (aged twenty-seven) resided at 10 Newton Street, Retford.

Frank Bennett has no known grave and is commemorated on the Menin Gate Memorial, Belgium.

PRIVATE ERNEST S MORTON

18449 8th Battalion King's Own Yorkshire Light Infantry.
Died 20th June 1916.

Pte Ernest S Morton died from wounds in France. He was the son of Mr and Mrs Morton, 41 Albert Road, Retford. The 1901 Census shows Ernest, aged twelve, living at the family home. Ernest's father James (b. 1853) is shown to be a tailor. As well as Ernest's mother Julia (b. 1850), there were two sisters and two elder brothers. His brothers - Harry (b. 1885) and Frank (b. 1886) – were employed as an iron-fettler and an apprentice iron-moulder respectively. The eldest daughter, Amy (b. 1882), was employed as a general domestic servant.

Ernest was with the 8th Battalion Kings Own Yorkshire Light Infantry when he died of wounds on 20th June 1916.

Abbeville was the headquarters for the Commonwealth Forces communications; it also housed a number of hospitals. It is likely that Ernest died in one of these hospitals.

Ernest is buried in Abbeville Communal Cemetery, France.

PRIVATE CHARLES GRANDE

9666 1st Battalion Lincolnshire Regiment
Killed 21st June 1916.

Report in the Retford Times
"The son of Mr Grande, Woolpack Street, Retford, has been killed in action. Pte Grande was a regular soldier and nineteen years of age. A brother, Joe Grande, was killed eighteen months ago, while his brother John Grande, also with the (6th) Lincolns, was seriously injured at Suvla Bay and has now been discharged. He is employed at Messrs Jenkins and Co. The gallant young lads made their home with Mr and Mrs F Guest of Wellington Street. Deep sympathy is felt with the relatives."

Charles Grande is buried in Ville-sur-Ancre Communal Cemetery, France.

PRIVATE HARRY TOMLINSON BIRKETT

1358 10th Battalion Lincolnshire Regiment.
Killed 1st July 1916.

Harry Birkett lived at North Cliff House, Kirton in Lindsey. Lincolnshire. His parents were John Nicholson and Emma Birkett. He attended Retford Grammar School, having entered in 1906. He was very sporty, having played football and cricket for the Grammar School 1st XI, when he left school in 1909 The Retfordian stated:

"In H Birkett the athletic side of the school has lost a shining light. On sports day he was ever conspicuous, and as a medium-paced bowler and a hard-working half-back, he held a leading place in our cricket and football teams."

"Harry Birkett was killed in action on 7 August 1916 [1 July according to CWGC]. He was in the Lincolns (Chums' Battalion). He fell in the Great Advance, wounded in the leg. His officer advised him to return, but with the spirit of a generous and brave soldier he did not wish to leave his comrades and decided to carry on. A little later, sadly, he was killed by the explosion of a shell. Harry was a great favourite with both officers and men, and was a splendid example to all around him."

Harry Birkett has no known grave and is commemorated on the Thiepval Memorial, France.

PRIVATE JOSEPH HENRY TURNER

14/104 14th Battalion York and Lancaster Regiment (Barnsley Battalion)
Killed 1st July 1916.

In 1901 Joseph Henry was living in Retford and working as a rubber sole maker, aged fifteen. His birthplace is indicated as being Barnsley and it is undoubtedly for this reason he joined the Yorks and Lancasters. His father, who had died by the time that Joseph was killed, had been employed in the railway cleaning house.

Prior to enlisting, Pte Turner had been employed at the Northern Rubber Works. He had been to Egypt with the Battalion and returned to France. Joseph's brother-in-law, Charles William Taylor, was killed on the same day, the first day of the Battle of the Somme, whilst serving as a Lance Corporal with the 12th Battalion of the Yorks and Lancasters (Sheffield City Battalion).

Joseph Turner has no known grave and is commemorated on the Thiepval Memorial, France.

PRIVATE WILLIAM MERRILLS
14385 11th Battalion Sherwood Foresters (Notts and Derby Regiment).
Killed 1st July 1916.

In July 1916 Mrs Merrills, mother of William Merrills, received a letter from Pte A W Morris saying, "I am sorry to have to inform you of the death of your son. We charged for the German front line, and when almost about three parts of the way we lay down for a wind. I had a look round and I saw Bill get struck on the head by a 'whiz-bang' which sent his steel helmet about 50 yards away. I crawled up to him and spoke, but I got no answer. He never moved again. It was very sad. It was a great shock to me. I thought of you and the kids. It was terrible. Then we got the order to charge, and off I went. When we got to the German front line there were six of us, a Corporal and a Major left. It was hell upon earth. They (the Germans) were even firing on our wounded as they were getting back to our lines. I don't know how I escaped it. I think I am very lucky, as I only got hit in the foot with a bit of shrapnel. It was not much of a wound, but just had enough, to get me back to England".

The objective on that fateful day for the 8th Division's 70th Brigade, of which 11th Sherwood Foresters (along with 8th Yorks and Lancs., 8th KOYLIS and 9th York and Lancs) were part, was Ovillers. The attack began at 7.30 a.m. with the 8th KOYLIS and 8th Yorks and Lancs in the first wave. While they made some progress, they met heavy fire from the Leipzig Redoubt to the north. With this heavy fire the attack lost some impetus, and the 9th Yorks and Lancs were sent into the affray but lost almost half of their men to machine gun fire in minutes. At 8.40 am the 11th Sherwoods were sent forward in two waves, with very few reaching the wire. It would have been during this attack that William Merrills would have been killed.

William Merrills has no known grave and is remembered on the Thiepval Memorial, France.

PRIVATE BERTIE S WOOLNER
18964 2nd Battalion Lincolnshire Regiment.
Killed 1st July 1916.

Bertie Woolner was the son of Alfred and Ellen Woolner, who lived at 4 Church Lane, Lowestoft. Bertie married Alice Maud and the couple lived at 49 Cobwell Road, Retford.

Bertie Woolner was a private in the 2nd Battalion Lincolnshire Regiment, which formed part of the 25th Brigade, which in turn was part of the 8th Division. The other battalions in the Brigade were the 2nd Royal Berkshire and the 2nd Royal Irish Rifles. On the 1st July 1916 the 25th Brigade left their assembly trenches to attack Ovillers, which lies just north of the Albert-Bapaume Road. Having been involved in heavy fighting at Neuve Chappell and being all regular soldiers, the 25th Brigade were seen as experienced and able to reach their objectives.

Below is an extract (written by an officer) taken from The History of the Lincolnshire Regiment

"As soon as the barrage lifted the whole assaulted. We were met with very severe rifle-fire and in most cases had to advance in rushes and return the fire. This fire seemed to come from the German second lines and the machine-gun fire from our left. On reaching the German front line we found it strongly held and were met with showers of bombs, but after a very hard fight about two hundred yards of German lines were taken about 7.50 a.m. Our support company by this time joined in. The few officers that were left gallantly led their men over the German trench to attack the second line, but, owing to the rifle and machine-gun fire, could not push on. Attempts were made to consolidate and make blocks, but the trench was so badly knocked about that very little cover was obtainable.

We were actually in the German trenches for two or three hours, and captured a lot more trench on our right by bombing as well as repulsing a German counter-attack from their second line. It was impossible to hang on longer owing to shortage of ammunition and no more bombs, as we had used up all our own as well as all the German bombs we could find in the trenches and dug-outs, and were being gradually squeezed out by their bombing attacks.

A company of the Royal Irish Rifles made a most gallant attempt to come to our support, but only ten or twelve men succeeded in getting through the zone of terrific machine-gun fire. We went into the attack with twenty-two officers, all of whom were killed or wounded, except Leslie and myself, and we had bullet holes through our clothing. During the time I had the honour of commanding the 2nd Battalion I never saw the men fight better; they were magnifi¬cent in the most trying and adverse conditions. The attack, though a failure, was a most glorious effort, and I was intensely proud of the battalion.

We first retired to shell holes in 'No Man's Land' and kept up fire on the trench we had left, with ammunition we collected from the wounded. As it was obvious we could do no good there, we retired to our own trench and reorganised to be ready for another attack if required. Orders were received from the 25th Brigade to withdraw Ribble and Melling Streets and occupy the assembly dug-outs, which was done."

Despite their efforts the 2nd Lincolns failed to take their portion of Ovilliers and the 25th Brigade was withdrawn, and it was during this attack that Bertie Woolner was killed.

Bertie Woolner is buried in Blighty Valley Cemetery, Authuille Wood, France.

PRIVATE CHARLES WOODWARD

32283 1st Battalion Sherwood Foresters (Notts and Derby Regiment).
Killed 5th July 1916.

"Pte Charles Woodward, Sherwood Foresters, was thirty-nine when he died. He lived with his sister, Mrs Crossland, at the Navigation Inn, Retford, and prior to enlistment (in October last year) was working in South Wales as a plasterer. His brother, Sergeant J Woodward, Inniskilling Dragoons, the old Retford footballer, was also doing his duty in France."

Charles Woodard has no known grave and is commemorated on the Thiepval Memorial, France.

PRIVATE JAMES CORDALL

21997 and Private Joseph (Joe) Lamb 15041 1st Battalion Sherwood Foresters (Notts and Derby Regiment).
Killed 5th July 1916.

Pte James Cordall and Pte Joe Lamb were in the 1st Battalion Sherwood Foresters, who were part of the 24th Brigade, 8th Division. The 1st Battalion Sherwood Forester did not take part in the major push of 1st July 1916 (the beginning of The Battle of the Somme). Having been in Rainneville, the Battalion moved to bivouacs in Henencourt Wood, just west of Albert on 30th June /1st July 1916. Whilst in Henencourt, a large number of soldiers from each company, plus officers and support troops, were told to be ready in the event of going into action. In all, this amounted to over 800 men and officers, whilst the rest were to remain in reserve. After three relatively quiet days in Henencourt Wood, the Battalion moved to Dernancourt on the River Ancre to the south of Albert. On 4th July at 8.30 p.m. orders were received to be ready at short notice in order to possibly support the 19th Division in a night attack. The Battalion set off at 10.30 p.m. The officers were of the opinion that they were to take over a line in La Boisselle and carry out some bombing raids the next day. While loading up with Mills bombs and Stokes mortar, the Battalion received orders that they were to attack on 5th July 1916 and consolidate the line taken.

The attack on the German line was difficult because officers of the Battalion had little time to do any reconnaissance, as their orders had changed considerably. In spite of 'D' company reaching its objectives, all companies were withdrawn to the original line by 9.00 p.m. At 2 a.m. on 6th July the Battalion was relieved and returned to their billets at Dernancourt. The battle was lost because of numerous factors, none more significant than this: as the 1st Sherwoods attacked their objective a regiment of Prussian Guards were moving up to the front to attack La Boiselle in order to retake the village, thereby giving numerical supremacy.

No figures are available for the number of casualties but they were heavy. Two known casualties were Pte James Cordall and Pte Joe Lamb. A special parade of the 1st Battalion Sherwood Foresters was ordered on 6th July 1916 by General Babington, Officer Commanding the 23rd Division, in recognition of the brave and gallant work carried out by the battalion.

Private Cordall was 24 years of age and prior to enlisting in January 1915, was employed at Messrs. Ashworths mill as a pickermaker. He had only been in been in France 10 weeks, when he met his death.

James Cordall is buried in Ovillers Cemetery, France.

Joseph Lamb, the son of James and Rebecca Lamb, was 29 years of age. He is buried in Serre Road Cemetery No. 2, France.

LANCE CORPORAL JAMES EDWARD NEWSTEAD
21241 12th Battalion Sherwood Foresters (Notts and Derby Regiment).
Died 8th July 1916.

James Edward Newstead was the son of Mr and Mrs. T Newstead, who lived at Canal Cottages (1901 Census). James's father, Thomas, originated from Broughton, Lincs, and was a porter on the canal at Retford Wharf, whilst his mother, Ellen, hailed from Farnsfield. James sustained wounds in action on 6th July 1916, dying on 8th July. James would have died in one of the numerous casualty clearing stations at Bailleul, which was an important railhead depot and hospital centre.

James Newstead is buried in Bailleul Communal Cemetery (Nord), France.

LANCE CORPORAL ALFRED SPENCER

24233 1st Battalion Sherwood Foresters (Notts and Derby Regiment).
Killed 15th July 1916.

Lance Corporal 24233 Alfred Spencer was reported in the Retford Times in August 1916 as missing; the Retford Times of 23rd March 1917 stated that Alfred was believed to be dead. The report states that Cpl Spencer was officially reported missing on 15th July 1916, having been in France only six weeks. He had enlisted in March 1915. The article went on to state that his wife, who lived at 15 George Street at the time of his death, had received information from the Minister for Pensions that the separation allowance (see appendix) she had been receiving would cease and she would receive a pension. The Minister in his letter wrote that the change of payment must not be taken as indicating that there was any proof of the death of her husband. Alfred left a widow and three children, who lived at 9, Poplar Street and his parents, who lived at 71, Albert Road. Prior to joining the army he worked for the Great Central Railway in Worksop. He was 29 years of age.

Alfred Spencer has no known grave and is commemorated on the Loos Memorial, France.

LANCE CORPORAL JOHN WOODWARD

14392 15th Battalion Sherwood Foresters (Notts and Derby Regiment).
Killed in 1st August 1916.

Although his death was recorded in the Retford Times of 16th February 1917, John Woodward was actually killed on 1st August 1916. Lance Corporal Woodward was the eldest son of Mr and Mrs J Woodward of West Street, Retford. The report in 1917 pointed out that Lance Corporal John Woodward had gone missing during fighting that took place on 1st August 1916. Prior to the war he was employed by the Retford Corporation. Sadly, the report states that John's wife died before the outbreak of the hostilities and with his death, two children, a boy and a girl, were orphaned.

On 14th September 1914 he underwent his training at Lulworth and Wool in Dorset, eventually embarking for France in June 1915. He was buried by a shell at Ypres and badly crushed and John spent some time in hospital in Sussex. Following his and convalescence he was returned to France in the early part of March 1916.

John Woodward has no known grave and is remembered on the Loos Memorial, France.

GUNNER JOHN THOMAS DUGDALE
32752 8th Division Ammunition Column, Royal Field Artillery.
Died 8th August 1916.

John's family originated from Selby in Yorkshire, where his grandfather, Thomas, lived and worked as a furniture dealer. His father moved to Moorgate in Retford, where he was employed as a painter and decorator.

Below is the report of John's funeral in the Retford Times:

"The funeral took place on Saturday afternoon at the Retford Cemetery of Gunner John Dugdale Trench Mortar Section, RFA, who, as briefly recorded in our last issue, died on the previous Tuesday in the Milton Military Hospital, Portsmouth as a result of wounds received in action. The deceased, who was 21 years of age, was wounded in the right knee by shrapnel on July 1st. He was a miner at Manton Pit, Worksop and enlisted at Retford in May 1915. He was sent to France last October. Mrs Dugdale visited her son in hospital at Portsmouth the week before he died. Her eldest son, Lance Corporal Lister Dugdale of the Seaforth Highlanders, has been in India since May.

A nurse at the Milton Hospital Portsmouth in a sympathetic letter to Mrs Dugdale wrote: "The night nurses and I have ordered some flowers to be sent to you on Friday. Will you kindly place them near him; he specially asked for roses the night before he passed away. It will be a very great consolation to you when I generally say that I sincerely hope when my time of parting comes I shall be as happy as he was: the vision of the angels and Christ stretching out his arms to take him home away from all his suffering is sufficient proof to me. He was quite conscious up to the end. I left him at 8.30 a.m. and he passed away about 9.30 am. I never left him at all that night. He was so bright and patient in spite of everything. He died a very happy death; in fact I have never seen a patient quite the same."

The Reverend M A Paxton, Vicar of St Saviour's Church, officiated at his funeral and the coffin was borne by six men of the RAMC, billeted in Retford. Some 120 members of the unit joined in the cortege. The last rites were of an impressive character and every manifestation of esteem and respect was shown for the late brave soldier."

PRIVATE FRANK MORLEY

4251 2nd Battalion Sherwood Foresters (Notts and Derby Regiment).
Killed 16th September 1916.

Frank was the son of Tom and Anna Morley, who lived at 32 Poplar Street, Retford. Frank enlisted at Derby in 1911 and was attached to the 4th Sherwood Foresters. Prior to enlistment Frank was employed as a groom.

Frank Morley has no known grave and is commemorated on the Thiepval Memorial, France.

PRIVATE FRED OSTICK

13611 2nd Battalion Sherwood Foresters (Notts and Derby Regiment).
Killed 16th September 1916.

Fred was the son of John and Mary Ostick, who resided at 25 Water Lane, Retford.

Fred Ostick has no known grave and is commemorated on the Thiepval Memorial, France.

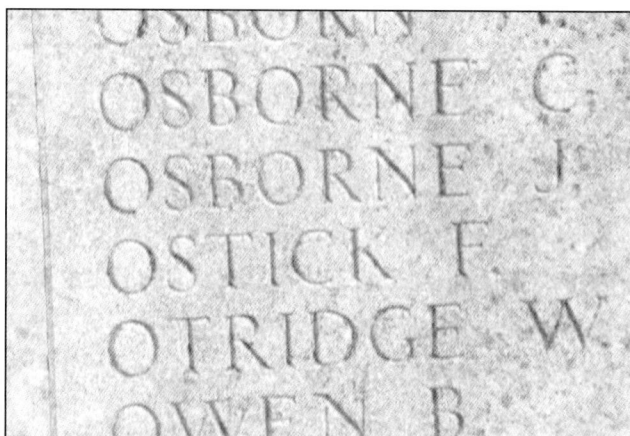

PRIVATE JOHN EDGAR HURST HIRST

10644 23rd Battalion Royal Fusiliers (1st Sportsman's)
Killed 16th September 1916.

John Edgar Hurst Hirst was the son of John Abraham Hurst Hirst, a local J.P., and Julia Caroline Hirst. The family resided at Moorgate Villa, Retford. Edgar was educated at the Retford Grammar School from 1887 and his name appears on the school's Roll of Honour. He joined as a private in the 29th Royal Fusiliers (University and Public School Battalion). On 19 March he went to Edinburgh for his training. He left for France in July, was transferred to the 23rd Royal Fusiliers (1st Sportsman's) and was killed 16th September 1916 by shell near Hebuterne.

John Hirst is buried in Euston Road Cemetery, Colincamps, France.

PRIVATE THOMAS HENRY COWLING

15137 9th Sherwood Foresters (Notts and Derby Regiment).
Killed in action on 23rd September 1916.

Thomas Henry Cowling was twenty years of age when he was killed in action. He was the son of James and Hannah Cowling, of Rayton Angles, Worksop. Thomas was born in Misterton and enlisted with the Sherwood Foresters in Retford.

Thomas Cowling has no known grave and is commemorated on the Thiepval Memorial, France.

PRIVATE ARTHUR SANDERSON

2261 1st /1st Nottinghamshire Yeomanry (Sherwood Rangers).
Died 24th September 1916.

Arthur was wounded fighting on the Macedonian front (also known as the Salonika front), which was formed as an attempt to aid Serbia.

Arthur Sanderson died of his wounds and is buried at Struma Military Cemetery, Greece, which was established near to the 40th Casualty Clearing Station.

SERGEANT FRED EDE DCM

12270 9th Battalion Sherwood Foresters (Notts and Derby Regiment)..
Killed 26th September 1916.

The 1901 census shows that Fred Ede, aged sixteen, was employed as a packer at the Northern Rubber Works, and lived at home at 9 Richard Street, Newtown, Retford, with his mother Elizabeth. Elizabeth was a widow at the time and employment shows her being a laundress, but out of work. Others living at home were May, aged twenty, also an unemployed laundress, Annie, aged fifteen, a dressmaker's apprentice, and Nellie, aged fourteen, also a dressmaker's apprentice. At the time of his death his mother was living at 59 Wharton Street.

Having survived Gallipoli and been awarded the D.C.M., Sergeant Fred Ede was killed in the later stages of the Battle of the Somme. He was killed on 26th September taking part on an attack on Joseph Trench and Schwaben Trench. The final objective was to be Hessian Trench, just to the south of Stuff Redoubt. The attack was part of the plan for the British to secure Thiepval Village, Stuff Redoubt, Schwaben Redoubt and St Pierre Divion.

Leading the assault on Joseph Trench were three companies of the 9th Sherwood Foresters and the 6th Border Regiment. With adrenalin running, the 9th Sherwoods moved too quickly and were caught up in the creeping barrage. Despite this setback, the attacking troops secured Joseph Trench with little loss of life. Leaving the Border Battalion behind to consolidate their gains and to mop up any resistance, the Sherwoods moved on Schwaben Trench. This also was taken and secured along with their section of Zollern Trench. In doing this, the Sherwoods took 200 prisoners and three machine guns. The three attacking companies were joined by the fourth company and moved on to their last objective, that of Hessian Trench. The 33rd Brigade, of which the 9th Sherwood Foresters were part, had achieved 90% of their objectives in this attack, but at a cost. Barry Cuttell in his book 148 Days on the Somme intimates that of the Brigade's 600 casualties most were from the 9th Sherwoods. Sadly, Fred Ede was one of them.

Fred Ede has no known grave and is commemorated on the Thiepval Memorial, France.

PRIVATE GEORGE ERNEST MORRIS
275872 Nottinghamshire Yeomanry (Sherwood Rangers).
Killed 7th October 1916.

Pte Morris was the son of William and Eliza Morris, who lived at 119 High Street, Ordsall. He was just twenty years of age when he was killed in action on the 7th October 1916.

From October 1915 to the end of November 1918, the British Salonika Force, of which the Sherwood Rangers were part, suffered some 2,800 deaths in action, 1,400 from wounds and 4,200 from sickness. The operations in Salonika brought very little success for the Allies, and none of any importance until the last two months. Any action taken by the Allies' forces was hampered throughout by widespread and unavoidable sickness, and by continual diplomatic and personal differences with Neutrals or Allies. On one front there was a wide, malarial river valley and on the other, difficult mountain ranges, and many of the roads and railways it required had to be specially constructed.

George Morris has no known grave and is commemorated on the Doiran Memorial, Greece.

SERGEANT JAMES TOMLINSON
26290 16th Battalion Sherwood Foresters (Notts and Derby Regiment).
Killed 10th October 1916.

'Sergeant James Tomlinson, third son of Mr and Mrs J W Tomlinson, 29 Chaplegate [25 Kirke Street, Retford according to the CWGC] is reported by the War Office as missing between 8th/10th October. He belonged to the Sherwood Foresters and joined in May 1915. The 16th Battalion was formed by the Duke of Devonshire and called the Chatsworth Rifles. He went to France in February 1916. Prior to enlisting in the army he was a member of the Notts Constabulary and was stationed at Arnold, Hucknall and Warsop. Prior to joining the police force, Sergeant Tomlinson was for six years with Mr V Woods, Mayfield, Retford.

James Tomlinson has no known grave and is commemorated on the Thiepval Memorial, France.

PRIVATE HAROLD MOTTASHED
27071 8th Battalion Loyal North Lancashire Regiment / 17th Battalion Manchester Regiment.
Killed 11th October 1916.

Harold Mottashed was the son of Walter and Agnes Mottashed, who lived at 17 Carolgate, Retford. He enlisted in September 1914 with the 8th Loyal North Lancs, but was actually with the 17th Battalion Manchester regiment when he met his death. On 11th October 1916, the 17th Manchesters were part of the 90th Brigade, which was pushing towards La Barque and onwards

towards Bapaume. It is likely that Harold was killed whilst moving up to the front line to replace the 41st Division.

The Census of 1901 shows that Harold's father, Walter, was employed as a draper's shopkeeper aged fifty, his birthplace being Retford. His mother Agnes, was thirty-nine and had been born in the West Indies in Montserrat.

Harold Mottashed has no known grave and is commemorated on the Thiepval Memorial, France.

PRIVATE FREDRICK WILLIAM BARBER
32533 5th Battalion Oxford and Bucks Light Infantry.
Killed 25th October 1916.

The parents of Fredrick had seven children, Frederick was the second youngest; the others were Robert, Stephen, Mary, Ernest, Elsie and Edith. The family lived at 35 Spa Common.

In February 1916 Frederick married Alberta Boshell in Leeds. The married couple lived in Beeston, Leeds. However, Frederick enlisted in Retford, originally joining the Notts and Derbys, and then moving to the 5th Oxford and Bucks Light Infantry. He was 28 when he died.

Fredrick Barber is buried in Agny Military Cemetery, France.

MAJOR CHARLES WALTER MERRYWEATHER
16th Battalion Lancashire Fusiliers.
Killed 23rd November 1916.

Charles Walter Merryweather was born on 31st May 1880, his mother and father lived at 19 The Square, Retford. Known as Walter, he attended Retford Grammar School. He visited France and Germany to gain experience in speaking their languages. This stood him in good stead when he went on to attend Trinity College, Cambridge, gaining an Honours degree in Modern Languages. Whilst attending university, Walter had gained a position as a teacher at Manchester Grammar School, living locally in Cheadle Hulme.

In November 1915 'A' Company of the 16th Battalion Lancashire Fusiliers went overseas with the rest of the Battalion, with Merryweather as their Company Commander. As Company Commander, he wrote to the Retfordian Magazine asking "Old Retfordians everywhere to supply a few pounds to supply his men with football boots, goal posts, draughts, dominoes, etc. The 250 men are mostly poor with 9 or 10 of them having to make allotments to their wives and dependants, and so draw on 3/6 per week (17.5p) for themselves out of which they have to pay insurance". The article goes on to say, "Other companies of better-class men have their complete outfits. £10 would be the means of keeping the men good and healthy and happy and keeping any amount from the default sheet". The first to subscribe was the Reverend Thomas Gough, Headteacher of the Retford Grammar School.

In the spring edition of the Retfordian it was reported that Walter Merryweather, whilst inspecting the trenches in January 1916, had been badly wounded by shrapnel/bullet in the thigh. The officer was in the frontline at Authile when he was wounded. The shrapnel/bullet was removed at a casualty clearing station followed by a 14-hour journey to No 2 Red Cross Hospital at Rouen. After a fortnight, Walter was back in England, spending time at a number of different hospitals. In May 1916 Walter received his first medical review whereby the authorities deemed him not to be fit enough to return to his battalion. Following a programme of graduated physical training, a month later Walter was passed fit by the medical board for foreign services. Whilst awaiting orders, Walter underwent a musketry course at Prestatyn.

Having rejoined his battalion, he was involved in November in one of the last actions of the Somme Battles of 1916. The attack was launched in poor weather conditions and troops began to withdraw to their original lines; however, a small group of soldiers from the 11th Border Battalion and the 16th Highland Light infantry was cut off in Frankfort Trench.

The plan was to send a party of around 320 men of the Lancashire Fusiliers and the Royal Inniskilling Fusiliers to retake Munich Trench and establish a foothold whereby a smaller party would attack Frankfort Trench in order to help the beleaguered soldiers of the Border and HLI Battalions. The attack was planned to take place on 23rd November 1916, with Walter Merryweather leading the attacking group.

Following a short British artillery barrage, the group charged out across no-man's-land towards Munich Trench; here they faced bombing from both ends of the trench they had taken. Fierce hand-to-hand fighting ensued, whilst a small group pushed forward towards Frankfort Trench. The party became pinned down, with both lieutenants having been shot. It was at this point that Walter could be seen standing on the parapet directing operations whilst calling the raiding party to return; this brave action proved fatal, as he was shot. The party which they had tried to rescue held on for a while longer, but having run out of water and ammunition they had to surrender. The Merryweather family received a telegram six days later about their son's death.

Charles Merryweather has no known grave and is commemorated on the Thiepval Memorial, France.

EDWARD BROUGHTON

14835 10th Battalion Sherwood Foresters (Notts and Derby Regiment).
Killed 31st October 1916.

On December 8th 1916 a letter arrived at Strawberry Villas, Newtown, Retford, the home of Benjamin and Annie Broughton, telling them that their son Edward had been posted missing following action which took place on 31st October 1916. The History of the 10th Battalion Sherwood Foresters by Lieut W N Hoyte states that the 10th Battalion were on their way up to the front on 30th October 1916 as part of the 17th Division, to replace the 8th division in the line opposite Le Transloy.

The conditions on the way up and in the trenches were very poor; Captain E.B. Joyce, with mud up to the waist, stated that the trenches were the worst they had experienced. In these conditions it was all the troops could do to stay in them for forty-eight hours. Consequently changes in the trenches were frequent.

It is highly likely that Edward Broughton was killed during one of these relief changes. Although Retford-born, Edward enlisted in Derby in September 1914. Before the war he worked as a clerk at Messrs W.J. Jenkins. He was educated at St Saviour's School. Edward was twenty-three years of age when he was killed and at the time of his death he had a brother, Benjamin Clarence Broughton, serving with the Sherwood Foresters and based in Ireland.

Edward Broughton has no known grave and is commemorated on the Thiepval Memorial, France.

PRIVATE GEORGE COOK

14906 Lincolnshire Regiment Depot.
Died 11th November 1916.

George Cook was only twenty-two when he died. He was the son of George Cook of 11 Beardsall's Row.

George Cook is buried In Eastbourne (Ocklynge) Cemetery in Sussex. Eastbourne was the site of a large Military Convalescent Hospital.

ABLE SEAMAN GEORGE GILBERT TAYLOR

T Z/4971 Royal Naval Volunteer Reserve, Hawke Battalion, Royal Navy Division.
Killed 12th November 1916.

George Taylor was nineteen years of age when he met his death towards the end of the Battle of the Somme. George was the son of Robert and Mary Taylor of 23 Moorgate, Retford. Prior to enlisting, George had been employed as an iron-moulder with the Great Northern Railway in Doncaster.

The date of death seems to point to the fact that AB Taylor received wounds whilst waiting for zero hour in the assembly trenches for the attack on Beaucourt Station, between Beaucourt sur Ancre and St Pierre Divion. Barry Cuttell, in his book '148 Days on the Somme', states "hostile fire caused casualties, Lt Colonel Saunders being killed whilst moving up to the assembly point."

George Taylor is buried in Warloy-Baillon Communal Cemetery, France.

PRIVATE CHARLES STOCKS

242312 1st/5th Battalion Northumberland Fusiliers.
Killed 14th November 1916.

The son of John and Mary Stocks, Private Charles Stocks died during the attack on the Butte de Warlencourt towards the end of the Battle of the Somme.

Charles Stocks is buried at Warlencourt Military Cemetery, along with Pte.Harry Cross, who died in the same attack. Harry Cross was an Old Retfordian who fought with the South African Brigade. The action began on 16th September 1916 and went through to 16th November 1916.

Entrance to Warlencourt British Cemetery, where Charles Stocks, as well as an old Retford School pupil, Harry Cross, who fought with the South African Brigade, are buried.

PRIVATE JOHN DIXON
35302 2nd Battalion King's Own Yorkshire Light Infantry.
Killed 18th November 1916.

John Dixon was the second son of Mr and Mrs Charles Dixon of 1, Turks Head Yard, Grove Street, Retford. Prior to enlistment in Wakefield, John had worked for the Gas Company and before that was employed as a postman in Gamston District. He left Retford in February/March 1914, and enlisted on 7th September 1914, which was his birthday.

Pte Dixon was shot in the left lung on 30th July 1915. He was evacuated through various casualty clearing stations and hospitals, then John spent time at St Leonards-on-Sea and Clacton-on-Sea recuperating.

Being deemed fit, he returned to France on 26th September 1916; twenty-two days later, on 18th November, he was reported missing. It was not for a further thirteen months that his death was confirmed. It was highly likely that Pte Dixon was killed in one of the last attacks of the Battle of the Somme, in the attack on Serre, which took place on Saturday 18th November 1916. The attack was said to be very reminiscent of the infamous attack on Serre on the opening day of the Battle of the Somme, except for the weather, which on 1st July 1916 had been scorching hot; on this day the men were advancing heads down into driving snow. Some of the attackers were seen in Serre, but lack of ammunition and exhaustion led to the attack's faltering.

John Dixon is buried in Serre Road Cemetery No 1, France.

PRIVATE JAMES WALTERS THEAKER
19993 3rd Battalion Grenadier Guards (attached to the 177th Tunnelling Company Royal Engineers).
Killed 11th November 1916.

James Theaker was born in Sutton on Trent. His next of kin is given as his cousin, Miss L. Walters, of Rampton.

James Theaker is buried in Vlamertighe Military Cemetery, Belgium.

CAPTAIN REGINALD PRINCE WINTOUR
Royal Engineers.
Died 15th December 1916.

Captain Reginald Prince Wintour was born in 1885 in Fylde, and was the second son of Francis Wintour. At the time of Reginald's death his father was manager of Great Northern Works at Doncaster. It would appear that Reginald, after being educated at Manchester Grammar School, followed in his father's footsteps and was a district superintendant on the Egyptian Railway systems. With the outbreak of war, Reginald gained a commission in the Army Service Corps (ASC). In December 1914 (taking effect from 30th November 1914) he was gazetted as a Temporary Lieutenant in the ASC. In May 1915 he was mentioned in the London Gazette, again as a Temporary Lieutenant (as a Staff Lieutenant for purposes of pay) with the ASC as a Railway Transport Officer (RTO). In November of that year he was transferred to the General List whilst still a Temporary Lieutenant with the ASC. The short obituary in The Times of 23rd December 1916 states that he was made Staff Captain when he was appointed as an RTO.

It would appear that Reginald saw service in France and Salonika. It was whilst serving in Salonika that he was taken ill and sent to Malta. From Malta he was invalided home, and died in Retford. Reginald was the nephew of Captain Charles Wintour, who lost his life on HMS Tipperary in the Battle of Jutland.

Reginald Wintour is buried in Retford Cemetery.

PRIVATE JOHN WILLIAM LACEY
57215 11th Battalion Sherwood Foresters (Notts and Derby Regiment).
Killed 23rd December 1916.

The Retford Times of 5th January 1917 reported the death of Pte J W Lacey, Sherwood Foresters. He was the son of Mrs Marshall of South Street, and was killed in action on 22nd December 1916 [23rd according to CWGC records].

Private Lacey had been an old Council School Boy and before enlisting was employed by Messrs Crossland, carters. In a letter received by his mother, an officer of the battalion stated: "Your son was a willing worker and a good soldier.

His death is keenly felt by both officers and men." Mrs Marshall's husband and another son were both wounded whilst serving with the colours.

John Lacey is buried in the Railway Dugouts Burial Ground (Transport Farm), Belgium.

1917

LIEUTENANT GEORGE CARMICHAEL HARRISON
6th Anti Aircraft Battery, 24th Heavy Artillery Group, Royal Garrison Artillery.
Killed 10th January 1917.

George Harrison is buried in Lussenthoek Military Cemetery, Belgium.

PRIVATE JOHN WILLIAM SPENCER
63761st/5th Battalion King's Own Yorkshire Light Infantry.
Killed 14th February 1917.

16th March 1917 announcement in the Retford Times of the death of John William Spencer

At the time of his death Pte Spencer was a soldier with the 1/5th Kings' Own Yorkshire Light Infantry. Having been formed in Doncaster in 1914, they were part of the 3rd West Riding Brigade, which in turn was part of the West Riding Division. By the time John had joined, the 1/5th KOYLIs was part of the 148th Brigade 49th West Riding Division. At the time of his death, John's parents (John and Martha Spencer) lived at The Carr, Retford; however, by the time his details were logged with the Commonwealth War Graves Commission his parents lived at 63, West Street. Again, as in so many cases, the parents were warned of his death before official notification arrived from the War Office, by a letter sent from a friend. The family also received a letter from Lord Derby, Secretary of State for War, stating that the "King commanded him to assure them of the true sympathy of the King and Queen, in their sorrow." The report in the Retford Times said "this gallant young hero, who has laid down his life for King and Country, was only nineteen years and ten months old".

Having received his education at the National School in Retford, Pte Spencer was employed as an apprentice in the butchering trade at the Retford Co-operative Store, followed by employment at Percy Frost's of Rotherham and Mr Skidmore of Moorhead, Sheffield. He enlisted on 26th September 1916 and John spent time at Clipstone Camp before embarking for France on 12th

January 1917. Before his embarkation, John was given, as many were, a short period of leave before leaving for Foreign Service. During his short leave he married Miss Revill, the daughter of Lance Corporal Revill, of Wright Wilson Street, on New Year's Day 1917. He died just six weeks later.

John Spencer is buried in Bellacourt Military Cemetery, Riviere, France.

ABLE SEAMAN JOHN ARTHUR DIXON
TZ/6386 Howe Battalion, Royal Navy Division, Royal Naval Voluteer Force.
Killed 19th February 1917.

On 19th February 1917 another "young Retford father laid down his life for King and Country", as reported in the Retford Times of 9th March 1917, in the person of Able Seaman John Arthur Dixon of the Howe Battalion, Royal Naval Division. He was the son of Mrs Dixon of 41 Moorgate and in 1913 married Miss Parkin of West Street. For a number of years he was employed at the Laundry on Grove Street, but shortly before the war went to work at a laundry in Hull and lived at 4 Glencoe Villas, Hull. He and his wife and child were in the first air raid at Hull, in June 1915. Possibly the Zeppelin raid affected John's decision to join, as he enlisted a month later in July 1915 and went to Crystal Palace, London, for training.

In November 1915 he was sent out to Egypt, and after being in the Dardanelles for seven months was invalided out with fever and a weak heart. He was in Greenwich Hospital for a month and afterwards spent a short time in August 1916 on leave in Retford. He went to France in November 1916 and had seen much heavy fighting. His death occurred on 19th February 1917 in a casualty clearing station, in France, from gunshot wounds received in the abdomen.

The Howe Battalion was in action in and around Miraumont on 17th February 1917 at the time of his death.It was likely that John Dixon was injured in the assault on a sunken road opposite Baillescourt Farm. Figures showed that he died with nineteen fellow soldiers and one officer from the Howe Battalion.

He left a wife and one four-year-old child..He had two brothers and two brothers-in-law serving with the forces: Pte Edward Dixon, Notts and Derbys, transferring eventually to the Royal Scots; Able Seaman Gunner William Dixon (regular in the Navy); his brothers-in-law Arthur Booth in the R E and Corporal Herbert Fisher in the Sherwood Foresters.

John Dixon is buried in Dernancourt Communal Cemetery Extension, which is 3 kilometres south of Albert, France.

PRIVATE HERBERT KAYE
43057 10th Battalion Sherwood Foresters (Notts and Derby Regiment).
Died of 2nd March 1917.

Herbert Kaye died of wounds whilst serving with 10th Sherwood Foresters. Prior to the war Herbert lived with his parents Mr and Mrs George Kaye in Alma Road, Retford. The report in the Retford Times described Herbert as a" bright, intelligent young man". Herbert received his education at the National School, later being employed at the Co-operative Stores. He enlisted in April 1916, being sent to France in October 1916.

Herbert Kaye died from gunshot wounds in a hospital in Rouen and is buried in St Sever Cemetery Extension, Rouen, France.

PRIVATE WILLIAM HOLLAND
15061 1st Battalion Sherwood Foresters (Notts and Derby Regiment).
Died 4th March 1917.

Further sadness arrived in Retford with the announcement in the Retford Times of the death of Pte William Holland, a regular soldier in the 1st Sherwood Foresters.

The 1901 Census has William aged sixteen living with his parents Mary Jane and Frederick, as well as four sisters and three other brothers. Sarah Ann was the eldest of his sisters.

William was the eldest of the sons, with a brother John who has the same birth year. The other siblings were Agnes, Mary Jane, Frederick and Susan. All the family are recorded as being born in Retford. Both John and Frederick Jnr went on to serve with the forces.

At the time of William's death the Times reports his parents as living at 1 Carr Road, Retford. (Commonwealth War Graves Commission have 100 Moorgate Hill, Retford; this may have been the address when correspondence between William's parents and the War Graves Commission was taking place in order to get details right when a permanent headstone was placed on William's grave).

William enlisted with the colours on 14th September 1914 and, following his training at Whitby Bay, moved to France on 16th May 1915. He was to be attached to the machine gun section and was thirty-two years of age when he was killed by a sniper, having seen a lot of action. As usual, the parents found out about William's death from a friend on 15th March 1917, followed by official notification from the War Office seven days later.

In late January 1917 the 24th Infantry Brigade, of which the 1st Battalion Sherwood Foresters were part, were ordered back to the Somme for its third tour of duty and it was not long before they found themselves in the trenches in the North Bouchavesnes sector. The Battalion's War Diary records "The battalion experienced the hardest frost it has ever known, on several nights there being 23 degrees of frost; water supply being hampered… It was impossible to carry out trench improvements as the hardness of the ground broke the pick shafts".

Men of the Sherwood Foresters on the march up to the front to take part in action in which Pte Holland was killed.

On 10th February 1917 the Battalion went back to camp near Bray and took part in some intensive training for what was to be action in and around St Pierre Vaast Wood. On March 4th 1917, with the assaulting troops in position by 2.00 a.m., the artillery barrage started at 5.15 a.m. However, there were several casualties as the Germans replied with their own artillery. The four companies of the 1st Sherwoods were attached to other battalions with specific tasks ranging from acting as carriers to that of "mopping up". By 6.15 a.m all objectives were achieved. At some stage during this action Pte William Holland fell victim to the German sniper.

William Holland is buried in Fins New British Cemetery, Sorel-le-Grand, France.

PRIVATE ARTHUR SLINGSBY

24200 10th Battalion Duke of Wellington's (West Riding Regiment).
Died 25th March 1917.

Obviously not all soldiers were killed in action or died of wounds: many soldiers succumbed to illnesses of varying kinds. One such soldier was Pte Arthur Slingsby. Arthur was the son of Mr and Mrs J E Slingsby of the Old Lodge, Babworth Hall, Retford.

Pte Arthur Slingsby was a member of the 10th Duke of Wellington's West Riding Regiment, having enlisted in Retford in March 1916, and was only twenty-five years of age when he died from pneumonia on 26th March 1917.

At the time of his enlistment Pte Slingsby was employed as a gardener at Park Hall, Mansfield, having previously worked at Osberton and Rufford Abbey. Following his training at Clipstone Camp, Pte Slingsby had been in France for seven months when his illness overtook him. The report in the Retford Times stated that he was a "man of very fine physique and a very popular football player.

When home on leave before going to the front he looked the picture of health and it was thought that he was quite equal to the stress and strain of the battlefield."

According to the report by his Company Quarter Sergeant Major, they had been on a march when he was taken ill. The family received a later dated 22nd March from the Sister in charge of the 3rd Canadian Casualty Clearing Station where he was being looked after, stating he was seriously ill, but assuring them that he was in a comfortable bed and the nurses and doctors present knew how to care for him. Sadly, he passed away on 25th March 1917; his parents received notification of his death on 2nd April 1917.

Arthur Slingsby is buried in Lijssenthoek Military Cemetery, Belgium.

PRIVATE SAM SANDERSON

36035 6th Battalion Leicestershire Regiment (formerly 57787 Sherwood Foresters (Notts and Derby Regiment)).
Died 6th April 1917.

Sam Sanderson was the son of Mr and Mrs J Sanderson of Spital Hill. In the 1911 Census he was show as living with his parents at 19 Wellington Street and was employed as a rubber spreader at the Northern Rubber Works. He was 30 years of age when he was killed in action.

Sam Sanderson is buried in Boyelles Communal Cemetery Extension, France.

CAPTAIN BENJAMIN CANNING HUNTSMAN

2nd/8th Battalion Sherwood Foresters (Notts and Derby Regiment).
Killed 7th April 1917.

Captain Benjamin Canning Huntsman was born on 26th April 1895.

In April 1917 Benjamin Huntsman's mother received a telegram to say that her 21 year old son, who had been serving as a Captain with the 2/8th Sherwood Foresters, had been reported missing. Benjamin was the son of Mrs Mary Huntsman and the late Mr Frank Huntsman who lived at West Retford Hall. The Huntsman family were descendants of Benjamin Huntsman, the inventor of crucible cast steel.

Following the German Retreat to the Hindenburg Line, from 14th March to 5th April 1917, on 7th April, the 2/8th battalion were based in and around the Flechin-Vendelles-Jeancourt and Le Verguier area (8-10 miles northeast of St Quentin). The diary for the 2/8th Battalion for this period tells us that the 2/7th Sherwood Foresters failed in their assault on Le Verguir (4th April 1917). This was followed by a failed attempt by the 2/5th Sherwood Foresters (5th April), and therefore the 2/8th were ordered to attack on 7th April, following artillery preparation. The Artillery caused damage to its own men. When the attack commenced, 'B' Company of the Battalion, commanded by Captain Huntsman, "got right on the wire, therefore suffering most casualties." It is thought that Captain Benjamin Canning Huntsman died in this action

Benjamin Huntsman has no known grave and is commemorated on the Thiepval Memorial, France

PRIVATE ARTHUR EDWIN HOWGATE

25449 2nd Battalion Lincolnshire Regiment.
Died 15th April 1917.

An account in the Retford Times of 27th April 1917 reported that the members of the families of Mr John Robert and Mrs Alice Howgate of 39 Moorgate Retford and that of Mr and Mrs Davies of Ollerton Road had attended services at Ordsall Church to pay their respects to Pte Arthur Edwin Howgate, who died on 15th April 1917.

The Davies family were his in-laws, Arthur having married Edith Davies on 24th September 1916. It would appear at the time of this report the Howgate family were not aware of the death of their other son, Alfred Thomas Howgate, who had been killed in action on 23rd April 1917.

Pte Arthur E Howgate, who was a member of the 2nd Battalion Lincolnshire Regiment, was severely wounded above the elbow of the right arm in action on 5th April. It would appear that he was not admitted to hospital in Rouen until 13th April 1917. On 14th April, the day after he was admitted, he was able to write a letter to his wife with his left hand, saying he would soon be home. It would appear that Pte Howgate succumbed to his wounds and exhaustion. His wife received notification of his death from wounds received in the same post as she received the last letter from her husband.

Before joining up, Arthur was employed by Mr Iremonger, Boot and Shoe Maker. Arthur was known locally as a good vocalist, winning prizes with a quartet at the North Notts Music Festival.

Arthur's wife, Edith, had two brothers serving; sadly, her brother Pte FW Davies, who was in the 1st Battalion KOYLI, died of wounds as Arthur had done, and by a strange turn of fate is buried in the same cemetery.

Arthur Howgate is buried in St. Sever Cemetery Extension, Rouen, France.

CORPORAL DAVID BELL

200994 1st/4th Battalion East Yorkshire Regiment.
Died 23rd April 1917

David was the son of D W Bell of 44 Grove Street, Retford. David served his apprenticeship as a pork butcher with J Thompson.

It would appear that David had his eye on travel, as he was employed as an engineer with a shipping company based in Hull at the outbreak of war. He enlisted in January 1915 and after three month's training embarked for France.

He was posted as missing in April 1917 with final confirmation of his death coming later in the year. Two years previously he had been reported missing but was found and he rejoined his regiment. He was 25 year old when he dies.

David Bell is buried in Wancourt British Cemetery, France.

LANCE CORPORAL ALFRED THOMAS HOWGATE
12253 16th Battalion King's Royal Rifle Corps.
Killed 23rd April 1917.

Alfred Howgate was the second of two sons of John and Alice Howgate, of 39 Moorgate, to die in France in April 1917. Like his brother, Arthur, who had died just eight days earlier, Alfred had worked as a shoe repairer for a Mr Iremonger before joining up.

Alfred Howgate has no known grave and is commemorated on the Arras Memorial, France.

PRIVATE MARK STANLEY
6013 8th Battalion Lincolnshire Regiment.
Killed 24th April 1917.

Mark Stanley was the youngest of seven brothers (three others served). Before enlisting, he worked at Marshall's in Gainsborough as a moulder. He enlisted in September 1914, having been rejected three times. He went to France at the end of 1915 and was killed by a shell.

Mark Stanley has no known grave and his name is commemorated on the Arras Memorial, France.

PRIVATE WILLIAM RICHARDSON
10678 2nd Battalion Lincolnshire Regiment.
Killed 28th April 1917.

William was the son of Mrs A Welch, who had remarried following the death of her husband. They lived at 63 Albert Road, Retford. William was twenty-five when he was killed. Prior to enlisting in September 1914, he worked for Mr Broadberry, Provisions Supplier. With the closure of the business, William went to work at the Northern Rubber Works. He had been in France sixteen months when he was killed.

William's Company Commander wrote to his mother, saying that "It is with the deepest regret that I write to inform you of the death of your son. He was killed April 28th (1917) by a shell. He was nicely buried and a cross was put up to mark the place. His grave has been registered. He always showed himself to be a good soldier, carrying out his duties with the greatest of steadiness and courage. His loss is very much felt in the Company. Please accept my sincerest sympathy in your great trouble".

William Richardson is buried at Heudicourt Communal Cemetery Extension, France.

LANCE CORPORAL HERBERT CRISP
202503 2/4th York and Lancaster Regiment.
Killed 3rd May 1917.

The 22nd June 1917 The Retford Times reported the death of Lance Corporal Herbert Crisp. Herbert had been reported missing on 3rd May 1917 and this was finally accepted as the date of his death. He was just twenty. This battalion had been formed in Sheffield on 21st September 1914 - hence they were known as the Hallamshires.

Herbert worked at Messrs Cash and Co for eight years before his enlistment in the army in December 1915. He was drafted to France in January 1916 and was attached to a Lewis Gun Team. Herbert was the son of Frederick Crisp, who at the time of his son's death resided at 14 Cosgrove Street, Cleethorpes.

Herbert had been brought up by his grandparents and lived at 4 Bescoby Street, Retford. He had been a member of the East Retford Church Recreation Room and had at one time been a member of the church choir.

Herbert Crisp has no known grave and is commemorated on the Arras Memorial, France.

PRIVATE CHARLES HENRY KIRTON
48735 13th Battalion The King's (Liverpool) Regiment, formerly 46742 Sherwood Foresters (Notts and Derby Regiment).
Killed 3rd May 1917.

Charles Kirton is shown on the 1911 Census as a farm labourer living with his parents, George and Ann Kirton, at 15 Spital Hill.

He has no known grave and is commemorated on the Arras Memorial, France.

PRIVATE CHARLES MILLINGTON
47977 18th Battalion West Yorkshire Regiment (Prince of Wales's Own).
Killed 3rd May 1917.

According to records, Pte Millington was born and enlisted in Retford. He was killed in action on 3rd May 1917, during the Third Battle of the Scarpe (part of the Battle of Arras).

Charles Millington has no known grave and is commemorated on the Arras War Memorial.

PRIVATE FRANK BETSON
201909 2nd/5th Battalion West Yorkshire Regiment (Prince of Wales's Own).
Died 5th May 1917.

Before the war, Pte Betson was a journeyman pork butcher, and in 1901 lived at 10 Carolgate with his employer, James Thompson, Pork Butcher, and the Thompson family, one other apprentice butcher and a servant - in all, twelve people. Following his time at Thompson's, Frank was employed for some time at the Retford Co-operative Society, and before he enlisted was foreman at Messrs. Nessells of Lincoln in their Butchery Department. He had a twin brother, Richard, who was landlord of the Black Boy, Moorgate.

Having enlisted in February 1916, he was taking part in the big push (Battle of Arras 1917) when he received shrapnel shot to the head.

He was returned to Lincoln Hospital, where he regained consciousness after six weeks of lying there, but had a relapse and died at the age of 41..

Frank Betson was buried in East Retford Cemetery with full military honours, his coffin being placed on a gun carriage drawn by six horses. The firing party was made up of East Anglian Engineers based in Retford. The service was carried out by the Vicar of East Retford, the Reverend C Bailey.

GUNNER HORACE PALETHORPE
38398 Royal Garrison Artillery, 3rd Arm Pool.
Killed 16th May 1917.

The Commonwealth War Graves commission records tell us that Horace was a member of the Royal Garrison Artillery 3rd Army Pool; this could indicate that he could have previously been wounded and had returned to service following convalescence, or may have been a volunteer, attested under the Derby Scheme, or a conscript and was part of a pool waiting to be placed in a certain battalion or awaiting a specific task. A fellow researcher has pointed out that Horace is buried in the middle of six other members of the 51st Brigade Royal Field Artillery and one of the 8th Siege Battery Royal Garrison Artillery, all of whom were killed on the same day. It is feasible that Horace may well have been attached to one of these units whilst officially with the 3rd Army Pool.

Gunner Palethorpe was born in Retford in 1893 and was the son of Daniel and Mary Ann Palethorpe, of 10 Leigh Street, Attercliffe, Sheffield, and the older brother of Lance Corporal Jim Palethorpe of the 2/5th Duke of Wellington's (West Riding Regiment), who was to die on 27th November 1917.

Horace Palethorpe is buried at Feuchy British Cemetery, France.

SERGEANT WILLIAM HILEY STAFFORD WALKER

82006 15th Battalion Sherwood Foresters (Notts and Derby Regiment).
Killed 16th May 1917.

Records show that William was the stepson of Mr W C Wightman of 13 Thomas Street, Retford. A book entitled The Blast of War: A History of the Nottingham Bantams' 15th Service Battalion Sherwood Foresters 1915-1919 by Maurice Bacon and David Langley tells us that the Sherwoods were involved in a substantial night raid on the evening of 15th/16th May 1917 in and around Gricourt, just northwest of St. Quentin. It is likely that William was killed during the raid.

William Walker has no known grave and is commemorated on the Thiepval Memorial, France.

PRIVATE ALBAN OFFORD

242606 1st/6th Battalion Sherwood Foresters (Notts and Derby Regiment).
Killed 3rd June 1917.

Pte Offord enlisted in 1914 and was killed at the age of 21. He was the son of Robert and Alice Offord, of 7 Storcroft Road.

Alban Offord is buried in Fosse No 10 Communal Cemetery Extension, Sains-en-Gohelle, France.

Above is a picture of the grave of Alban Offord (aged twenty-one) before the Portland Stone headstones were used. To the right is the grave of Sergeant W. Booth (aged twenty-six), the son of Thomas Henry Booth, of Upper End, Peak Dale, Stockport, who was killed on the same day. To the left is the grave of Pte Harry Fuller (aged twenty-six), from Newmarket, Suffolk, also killed on 3rd June 1917.

PRIVATE JOHN HEMPSHALL

63038 2nd Battalion Sherwood Foresters (Notts and Derby Regiment).
Killed 1st July 1917.

Born in Rotherham, John's family moved to 61 Wharton Street, where his widowed father lived at the time of his death.

John Hempshall has no known grave and is commemorated on the Loos Memorial, France.

PRIVATE JOHN COOLING 48679

13th Battalion The King's (Liverpool Regiment), formerly 51635 Sherwood Foresters (Notts and Derby Regiment).
Died 7th July 1917.

Pte Cooling was the son of Mrs Cooling, who had lived at 27 Kirke Street, prior to moving to Gainsborough with her son William. John is shown as having been born in Ordsall. John's father, who was deceased at the time of his son's death, had been a signalman at Thrumpton Lane Crossing. John had been on active service for seven months when he died of wounds. Prior to enlistment in Retford, John Cooling worked as a driller for Messrs Jenkins.

John Cooling is buried at Grevillers British Cemetery, France.

PRIVATE JOHN (JACKIE) BREDDY

26096 2nd Battalion Wiltshire Regiment, formerly 3/25491 Lincolnshire Regiment.
Died 12th July 1917.

The Retford Times of 20th July 1917 reported that a full military funeral had been held at Retford Cemetery for John (Jackie) Breddy on 16th July 1917.

He was buried with full military honours following his death at a Military Hospital in Manchester. John had succumbed to serious head wounds received in action whilst with the 2nd Battalion Wiltshire Regiment. Pte Breddy had originally signed up with the Lincolnshire Regiment, being transferred to the Wilts on being sent out to France. Pte Breddy was twenty years of age at the time of his death, and had previously been employed at the Carr Foundry, Retford.

John's mother, Elizabeth, lived at 19 Spital Hill.

John Breddy is buried in East Retford Cemetery, Retford.

PRIVATE HENRY TALBOT
203262 1st/4th Battalion King's Own Yorkshire Light Infantry.
Killed 19th July 1917.

Pte Talbot was the son of William and Diana Talbot, who lived at 1 Spurs Cottage, Churchgate, Retford. He enlisted in Bridlington and was aged thirty when he died.

Henry Talbot is buried in Coxyde Military Cemetery, Belgium.

PRIVATE COLIN WILLIAMS
98661 51st Company Machine Gun Corps.
Died 26th July 1917.

In 1911 Colin Williams was living with his grandfather, James Taphouse, mother, Sarah Ellen Williams and brother, Alfred, at 18 Albert Road, Retford. At the time Colin was an office clerk at a local brewery.

Colin married Mercy Wilson, a cook from near Tunbridge Wells, in East Retford in 1914. Her address given by the Commonwealth War Graves Commission, was Cares Cottage, Boar's Head, Tunbridge Wells, Kent. Pte Williams enlisted in Retford. The 51st Machine Gun Company were part of the 51st Brigade, 17th (Northern) Division, and served alongside 7th Lincolnshires, 10th Sherwood Foresters, 8th South Staffs, 7th Borders and 3/4th Royal West Kents.

Pte Williams died of wounds, probably at 8th Casualty Clearing Station.

Colin Williams is buried at Duisans British Cemetery, Etrun, France.

CORPORAL LEONARD BRIGGS
18667 1st Sherwood Foresters (Notts and Derby Regiment).
Killed 31st July 1917.

Private Harry Sutton 18588 1st Sherwood Foresters (Notts and Derby Regiment).
Killed 31st July 1917.

Having been stationed in and around Ypres for the most of June (the Battalion's first experience of the Salient), the 1st Sherwood Forester's moved to Beaumetz-les-Aire to carry out training for a forthcoming attack, which became known as the Third Battle of Ypres, more commonly known as Passchendaele.

It was during this battle that both men were killed.

Leonard Briggs was the son of Thomas, a market gardener, and Matilda Briggs of Clarborough.

Harry Sutton was the son of Mr and Mrs John Sutton of 71 West Street in Retford. His brother Jack was to die in hospital in 1918, having served with the Royal Navy..

Neither man has a known grave and their names are commemorated on the Menin Gate Memorial in Ypres, Belgium.

PRIVATE JACK (JOHN) PARKIN
53285 17th Battalion Sherwood Foresters (Notts and Derby Regiment).
Killed 30th July 1917 [4th August 1917 according to CWGC].

'Mrs Parkin, 12 Spa Lane Retford, who was married to Arthur Parkin (employed by Messrs. Hurst and Son, Builders and Joiners, Corporation Wharf, Retford), heard that the eldest of her three sons serving in the war had made the great sacrifice in July.' Retford Times.

Jack was aged thirty-six, and serving with the 17th Service Battalion (Welbeck Rangers) Sherwood Foresters. He lived with his wife and two children on Moorgate. After his death his wife moved to live with her parents in Rotherham. He joined the colours in June 1916 and had been in France for about nine months. He was an old scholar of the Retford National School and before the war was employed by Mr William Crossland, Coal Merchants, Grove Street, Retford. Mrs Parkin's other two serving sons were Pte Fred Parkin (twenty-six at the time of the report), who had been serving nearly three years and was formerly employed in the Carr Foundry, and Pte Arthur Parkin, who was called up July 1917 and was in training at Sunderland.

Pte John Parkin is buried at Track X Cemetery, Belgium.

LIEUTENANT ARTHUR AARON ENDERBY
4th Battalion Royal Fusiliers (City of London Regiment)
Died 2nd August 1917.

A former pupil of Retford Grammar School, Arthur Enderby. He enlisted at the outbreak of war in the 4th Battalion Bedfordshire Regiment and obtained his commission in November 1914.

His commanding officer wrote to his parents:
"Allow me to express the deep sympathy of all ranks of the Royal Fusiliers at the loss of you gallant son. He had made himself very popular with both officers and men. I found him an excellent officer, absolutely reliable, who knew his work and did it well. At the time he was wounded he was in command of an isolated post, a nasty job calling for pluck, self-reliance and initiative, all of which he showed in a marked manner. Officers like your son cannot be spared."

He died of wounds, received in action on 25th July 1917, at the 3rd Casualty Clearing Station.

Arthur Enderby is buried in Grevillers British Cemetery, France.

PRIVATE GEORGE OSTICK
43268 9th Battalion Princess Victoria's (Royal Irish Fusiliers), formerly 13009 Sherwood Foresters (Notts and Derby Regiment).
Killed 16th August 1917.

Private George Ostick was the son of Mr and Mrs Harry Ostick of 25 Water Lane, Moorgate. He was reported missing in action on August 16th 1917, with official news arriving in February 1918. He died whilst serving with the Princess Victoria 9th Battalion Royal Irish Fusiliers having originally enlisted with the Sherwood Foresters in Retford. George went into battle with 'D' company.

The Battalion War Diary, transcribed by Andy Shaw, a Great War Forum Member, reads:

''At zero hour (4.45am) the battalion attacked. Our left flank was in touch with the left flank of the 7/8th Royal Irish Fusiliers. We advanced from the old trench running between Pommern Redoubt to Iberian Farm and opened fire after advancing 50 yards, with rifles, Lewis guns and rifle grenades. As we approached Hill 35 the enemy opened fire and each company merged due to heavy casualties, Machine gun fire from hill 35 held up the advance for 20 minutes in which time the 7/8th Irish Fusiliers had got ahead of us.

When hill 35 was taken one platoon was detached to consolidate it and the remainder pushed on until it reached a double row of wire south east of Gallipoli Farm. This held up the advance. Heavy machine gun and rifle fire was brought to bear on us from dugouts etc. in Gallipoli and long range machine gun fire from the direction of Aisne House, Martha House and Hill 37.

Casualties were very heavy now and it was impossible to push on and the position outside wire at Gallipoli was untenable so we retired back to hill 35.

The resistance encountered was very stubborn and the enemy only retired when almost surrounded, very few allowed themselves to be taken prisoner. They fought until practically until every man was killed on Hill 35.

Our casualties killed in action 36, wounded 323, shell shock 12, missing 83 and missing believed killed 2."

Details on the casualty return for that day reports George missing, gives his wife's name as Mary and his address as 5 Spa Lane, Retford.

George Ostick is buried in New Irish Farm Cemetery, Belgium.

SECOND LIEUTENANT REGINALD WILLIAM CLARK
3rd Battalion Sherwood Foresters (Notts and Derby) Regiment.
Killed 19th August 1917.

Reginald Clark, of 13 Alma Road, had served with the Sher¬wood Rangers as a Sergeant since 1914, in Egypt and Salonika. During the great retreat from Serbia he served in that country with a Machine Gun Section. During the early days of the war he won the certificate from the Royal Humane Society for saving Sgt. Hill of Torworth from drowning. He was granted a commission in the Sherwood Foresters, but was killed in action on 19th August 1917. "He was brave and considerate in all things at all times, is the verdict of those who knew him best."

Reginald Clark is buried in Woods Cemetery, Belgium.

CORPORAL ALFRED BROWN
267466 1st/6th Battalion Sherwood Foresters (Notts and Derby Regiment).
Killed 26th August 1917.

The son of Henry and Sarah Ann Brown of the Osborne Vaults, Carolgate, and the husband of Levina, Alfred was 35 years of age when he was killed in France. In the 1911 Census he is shown as a self-employed cooper living at 53, High Street, Ordsall.

Alfred Brown is buried in Sailly-Labourse Communal Cemetery Extension, France.

PRIVATE HAROLD WILLIS
41312 10th Battalion Lincolnshire Regiment.
Died 26th August 1917.

Mr and Mrs Frank Willis at Glebe Farm, North Road, Retford, received Information in mid- September that their youngest son, Pte Harold Willis, had made the greatest sacrifice.

The news came from a comrade in hospital in Bridgenorth, Shropshire, who stated in his letter that on 26th August 1917 a large number of soldiers were buried alive and only three of them escaped with their lives. The soldier who wrote the letter was one of the three.

The deceased, who was only nineteen years of age, was called to the colours on 7th January, his father's birthday, and was trained at Brockton Camp. He went out to France in the second week of May 1917. He was described as being quiet and willing. The report in the Retford Times stated that "he had never been away from home until he received his call-up papers."

Harold, along with his four brothers, attended the National School in Retford and also attended the West Retford Baptist Sunday School.

Harold Willis has no known grave and is commemorated on the Thiepval Memorial, France.

SECOND LIEUTENANT DAVID TANNER

8th Battalion Sherwood Foresters (Notts and Derby Regiment).
Kelled 30th August 1917.

Lieutenant David Tanner, 8th Notts and Derbys Regiment, was initially reported missing after a reconnaissance expedition on the French front during the night of August 29th. Eventually the young officer's name was included in an official list from Germany, and his father, Mr. David Tanner, of Retford, received a report from the War Office that "the death of Second Lieutenant D. Tanner has been officially accepted as having occurred on, or shortly after, 30th August, 1917."

David Tanner enlisted on 1st September 1914 as a private and is credited with getting a number of Retford lads to join, including his brother, Harold. His promotion through the ranks was speedy and he soon found himself as a Sergeant. Having spent two years' hard fighting in France, he was offered a commission and returned to England to train with the Officer Cadet Corps. On receiving his commission he returned to France and was attached to the 1/8th Sherwood Foresters.

It was only four weeks later that he went missing whilst leading a small raiding party. Captain W.C.C Weetman's The Sherwood Foresters in the Great War 1914-1919: 1/8th Battalion states that Lieutenant David Tanner "very gallantly undertook to reconnoitre a Boche post, and took out with him Corporal Harry Wright (also commemorated on the Loos Memorial) and two men. The two men got back safely, but Tanner and the NCO were missing, and were reported later to have either been killed or to have died of wounds." A report in the Retford Times stated that "he was a young man of brilliant attainment, and there is no doubt that, if spared, he would have made a name for himself in the scholastic world".

He started his schooling at the Council School in Retford and attained a junior scholarship, whereupon he attended the Grammar School. He finished at the Grammar School in 1911 and went to London University, where he gained his Inter BA. He then went to Sheffield University to continue his studies, and took up teaching as an Assistant Master at a school in Kent.

He was remembered as a magnificent swimmer, and was champion in swimming and diving two years in succession (1909 and 1910) at the Grammar School. He was also a prominent member of the Retford Swimming Club.

David Tanner has no known grave and is commemorated on the Loos Memorial, France.

GUNNER SAMUEL WARDLE
186046 380th Battery, 158th Brigade, Royal Field Artillery.
Killed 4th Sept 1917.

Gunner Samuel Wardle's father, also named Sam Wardle, was a well-known member of the Retford Volunteer Corps. Samuel and his wife, Selina, at the time of the report of their son's death lived at 21 Wright Wilson Street, Retford. Samuel Jnr was their third son, and was with the Royal Field Artillery when he was killed on 4th September 1917. The officer commanding his battery, Captain Godwin, in a letter sent to his parents stated: "I am very sorry to have to inform you that your son was killed in action on the 4th of this month. At the time of his death he was doing excellent working on a gun pit, which was on fire. He was buried in the cemetery close by, and I am having a suitable cross placed over his grave. Once again expressing my sympathy in your bereavement".

Samuel Wardle was joined up in November 1916. Following training, he went to France on 4th June 1917. Before the war he was a driller at Messrs. W J Jenkins and Co Ltd, having previously been employed at the Northern Rubber Works.

His brother, Wheeler T H Wardle, also of the RFA, who lived at 31 Wright Wilson Street, had been in France for a year at the time of the report of Samuel's death; he had also been employed at the Rubber Works where his father had worked for many years. Several weeks before Samuel's death, another brother, Trooper Ingle Wardle, who was with the Sherwood Rangers, survived when a ship that he was travelling on was torpedoed.

Samuel Wardle is buried in Coxyde Military Cemetery, Belgium.

PRIVATE WALTER CECIL RANDALL
305324 1st/8th Sherwood Foresters (Notts and Derby Regiment).
Killed 12th September 1917.

Walter Randall's death was confirmed in the Retford Times on 28th September 1917 under the headline "Retford Soldier Family, Grandson of an Old Volunteer":

'As intimated last week, Pte Walter Randall, Sherwood Foresters Lewis Gun Section, was killed in action on the night of the 12th inst. He was the second son of Mr and Mrs E Randall of 1 Beardsall's Row, Retford, grandson of the late Sergeant H Brown, Osborne Vaults, (who served in the old Retford Volunteer Corps for half a century), and nephew of Sergeant A Brown, Ordsall, whose death was recorded a fortnight ago. Pte Walter Randall, who was in his 21st year, was a month ago on leave in Retford with Pte

George West, Thrumpton Lane, and Pte Clark, and returned to France August 21st. It will be recalled that the deceased's brother, Pte Harry Randall, made the great sacrifice over two years ago, and another brother, George, has recently joined the colours. '

Pte George West, in a letter to the bereaved parents, says, 'I hope you can bear the sad news as well as you can. Your son's death made me very ill as we were such big pals. I cannot tell exactly how it happened, but I know he felt no pain. A large number made the great sacrifice including (Cyril) Parkin from Hayton, (George) Darwin from Clayworth, Billy Bell, Ordsall, who had his legs blown off and was still alive when he was carried out of the trenches. We have lost one of the best lads in the battalion in Walter who was liked by everyone who knew him. He was always willing to do anything set before him. Much sympathy is felt by all the Retford lads in the great loss of your dear son.'

Other letters have been received from Pte Clark, who states 'I have lost one of my best pals when I lost Walter'. Pte A N Scott (in a London hospital) refers to the deceased as 'a good honest and straightforward soldier' and says that the loss of his great friend is 'another example of fine young life lost in endeavour to uphold righteousness and national honour'. 'Your son was a good soldier and will be greatly missed by everyone in his company: he was cheerful under all circumstances and a general favourite wherever he went,' writes Lieutenant Elly (himself to die in September 1918, aged twenty-four).

Like his brothers, Pte Walter Randall joined the Retford Territorials when he was seventeen years of age. He was an old National School boy and was in the employ of Mr W Mottashead of Carolgate (who lost a son, Harold, in 1916) and in the loco department of the Great Northern Railway. Mr and Mrs Randall have received a large number of letters of sympathy."

The action in which Walter was killed also took the lives of Cyril Parkin, George Darwin and Willie Bell as well as six others. They were subject to a bombardment on the night of 12th September 1917, following an unsuccessful raid the previous night.

Walter Randall has no known grave and is commemorated on the Loos Memorial, France.

PRIVATE GEORGE OSWALD DARWIN
305636 1st/8th Sherwood Foresters (Notts and Derby Regiment).
Died 13th September 1917.

George Oswald Darwin was born in Clayworth The 1911 Census shows that he had 13 living siblings. His parents were George, a gardener, and Mary Darwin, of Mill House, Clayworth.

George was twenty-two years of age when he died of wounds, following the same incident that claimed the lives of Walter Randall and William Bell.

George Darwin is buried Cambrin Military Cemetery, France.

PRIVATE WILLIAM (WILLIE) SMITH BELL
305322 1st/8th Sherwood Foresters (Notts and Derby Regiment).
Died 14th September 1917.

Willie Bell (also known as Billy Wilkinson because he had lived with his brother-in-law, David Wilkinson, in Birketts Row in Ordsall), was born in Saxilby, Lincolnshire, but enlisted in Yorkshire. He is shown as an iron founder in the 1911 Census.

He died of wounds following the same incident that claimed the lives of Walter Randall and George Darwin. A report in the Retford Times states that he was at his front post when he was severely wounded in the legs on the night of 12th September 1917. His Lieutenant (E J Elly who was to be killed later in the war in 1918 aged twenty-four years) wrote that "He was unconscious from the first. Everything possible was done for him, but the shock evidently proved too much for his constitution and he passed away in the 33rd Clearing Station (Bethune) on 14th September 1917. Had he lived, I am afraid he would have lost both his legs and been a helpless cripple." Lieut Elly goes on to say that "Private Bell was one of the best soldiers in my platoon and I can assure you he will be greatly missed."

Willie Bell is buried in Bethune Town Cemetery, France.

PRIVATE HERBERT CROSSLAND
70128 16th Battalion Sherwood Foresters (Notts and Derby Regiment).
Died 15th September 1917.

In the 1911 Census Herbert Crossland is shown living with his widowed mother, Ann, at 19 Canal Street, Retford. He was employed as a carter for W. Tanner, a coal merchant.

He died at the National General Hospital, in London, of wounds received in action. His next of kin is shown as his brother, W. Crossland of Beardsall Row, Retford.

Herbert Crossland is buried in East Retford Cemetery.

LANCE CORPORAL HERBERT SAUNDERS

8094 Machine Gun Corps, formerly 23685 Northumberland Fusiliers.
Killed 20th September 1917.

Lance Corporal Herbert Saunders had joined the 64 Machine Gun Corps (64th Brigade 21st Division) having previously enlisted in the Northumberland Fusiliers. He was the son of William Herbert and Phoebe Saunders, of Moorgate, Retford, and was just twenty-two years of age. His father was a general and marine storekeeper.

Herbert Saunders is buried in Tyne Cot Cemetery, Belgium.

PRIVATE MARK WALTER FUGUEL

27536 10th Battalion Royal Warwickshire Regiment, formerly 3400 Sherwood Foresters (Notts and Derby Regiment).
Killed 20th September 1917.

Known as Walter Fuguel, he was the son of James and Mary Fuguel of Bishopsthorpe, York. He was born in York in 1879. Prior to enlisting, Walter worked as a butler at West Retford Hall.

In a letter to his own mother in Water Lane, and published in the Retford Times of 5th October 1917, Private S Holland states, "I am sorry to say we have had another poor chap from Retford killed. I do not know if you know him or not - butler at West Retford Hall, Mrs Huntsman's, and his name is Fuguel. He had been there a good while. He joined the Notts and Derbys (his regimental number indicates he was in the 1/8th Sherwood Foresters) and came to us with the lot from Notts and Derbys. It is a bad job he got killed in the last push as he was a good chap in the trenches. There are only two of us left in the Warwicks from Retford". Pte Fuguel was thirty-eight when he died.

Walter Fuguel is buried at Tyne Cot Cemetery, Belgium.

PRIVATE ALFRED WELTON

66702 26th Battalion Royal Fusiliers
Killed 20th September 1917.

The 1911 shows Alfred living with his parents at 26 Wright Wilson Street. He was employed as a grocer's assistant. He married Millicent Footit in Retford in the spring of 1917. He was twenty-six years old when he died.

Alfred Welton has no known grave and is commemorated on the Tyne Cot Memorial, Belgium.

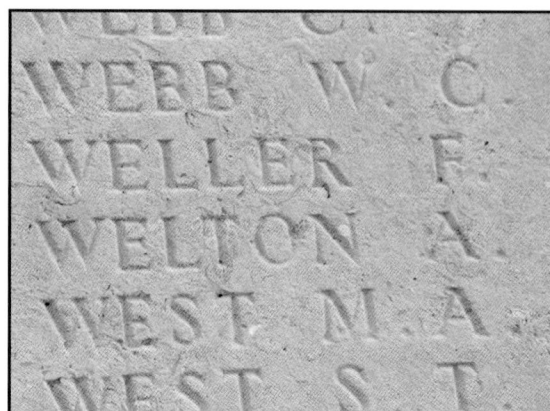

PRIVATE ARTHUR FULLARD

66535 32nd Battalion Royal Fusiliers.
Died 22nd September 1917.

Arthur was the son of Charles and Elizabeth Fullard of Little Gringley. The 1911 Census shows him working as a farm labourer in Laxton near Newark.

Arthur Fullard has no known grave and is commemorated on the Tyne Cot Memorial, Belgium.

PRIVATE GEORGE HENRY DUDDRIDGE

70776 2nd /5th (Sherwood Foresters Notts and Derby Regiment).
Died 26th September 1917,

Prior to the war George was employed as the second gardener at Blithfield Hall, Staffordshire. He enlisted in November 1915 and was a soldier with the 2/5th Sherwood Foresters at the time of his death. It was his brother, William T Duddridge, who first received the news of the death of George. William was the head gardener at Fairy Grove Nurseries, later T.J. Barker and Son, Retford. George's father, William Duddridge (born in 1849), came from Bridgewater, Somerset; he had been a canal agent and lived at the Wharf with the family. His mother, Ellen E Duddridge (born in 1853), was from Sheffield.

It is likely that George was killed at the start of the Battle of Polygon Wood on 26th September 1917, as the 59th Division were in action in this battle and the 2/5th Sherwoods were part of that division, being in the 178th Brigade. Prior to this action, the 2/5th Sherwoods were involved in the suppression of the Easter Rising in Ireland in April 1916. On returning to England in January 1917, they were soon on their way to France in February.

George Duddridge has no known grave and is commemorated on the Tyne Cot Memorial.

LANCE CORPORAL ALFRED NICHOLSON

270595 2nd Battalion Royal Scots, formerly Sherwood Foresters
Killed 26th September 1917.

The 1911 Census shows Alfred Nicholson living with his mother and stepfather, Edmund Layhe, at 1 Queen Street, Retford. He was employed as an ostler.

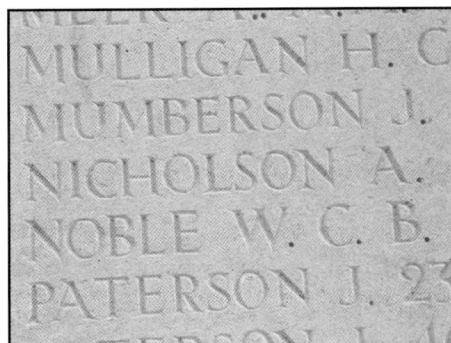

Alfred Nicholson has no known grave and is commemorated on the Tyne Cot Memorial, Belgium.

PRIVATE SYDNEY JACKSON
306512 2nd/8th Sherwood Foresters (Notts and Derby Regiment).
Killed 29th September 1917.

Sydney Jackson lived at 88 Ollerton Road, Retford. His parents, George and Ruth Jackson, came from Grantham and moved to Retford in 1910, initially to 16 George Street.

Sydney's parents received a letter from Captain Greaves, an officer of the 178th Light Trench Mortar Battery to which Sydney was attached. The letter stated: "I very much regret to inform you of the death of your son in action on 29th September 1917. He was killed instantaneously. His loss to me is very great as he was one of the original members of the battery and was always a willing and capable lad. Please accept my deepest sympathy in this your trouble. You may be sure his sacrifice is not in vain." Two other soldiers of the 2/8th Sherwoods attached were killed at the same time, and all are buried in White House Cemetery, St Jean-les-Ypres. They were Private Basil Webster, aged twenty-four, of 1 Market Place, Worksop, and Private Frank Selby, aged twenty-one, of 32 Whitfield Street, Newark.

The report goes on to say that the unit were leaving the trenches and congratulating themselves on having no casualties when an enemy aircraft dropped a bomb, killing the three men.

Pte Sydney Jackson, who was born in Leicester, enlisted in January 1916. He had received his training at Watford and Harpenden and at some stage trained with the trench mortars at Aldershot. Whilst home on leave, the Easter Rebellion started and Pte Jackson was dispatched to Ireland immediately.

Sydney Jackson is buried in White House Cemetery, St Jean-les-Ypres, Belgium.

PRIVATE STANLEY ADWICK
107779 112th Company Machine Gun Corps, formerly 2039 Nottinghamshire Sherwood Rangers Yeomanry.
Killed 8th October 1917.

In 1881 Stanley's parents were living at 128 Grammar Street, Nether Hallam, Yorkshire. Thomas, his father, was twenty-eight (born in Worksop), and recorded as being a tailor. Fanny, his mother, was aged twenty-one (born Retford, nee Tate). At this time they had one daughter named Ethel, eleven months old.

The 1901 Census shows Stanley Adwick, aged ten, living at Pennington Gardens, Retford, with his mother and father and six brothers and sisters. By 1911 he was employed as a butcher in Worksop.

Stanley Adwick's death in action on 8th October 1917, aged twenty-five, was announced in late October 1917 in the Retford Times. He joined up, on 5th October

1914, the Notts Sherwood Rangers Yeomanry and served with the regiment in Egypt and Salonika. He was invalided home from Greece and after recovery joined his unit at Aldershot. Here, with other Yeomen, he was transferred to the Sherwood Foresters (Robin Hoods) and was sent out with a draft to France on Christmas Eve 1916.

He was invalided home with malaria in April 1917, and was in hospital in Birmingham and Nottingham, spending a period of convalescence in Somerset. Then on 26th September 1917 Pte Adwick made a second journey to France, serving with the Machine Gun Corps, 112 Company. He had been at the front only about a fortnight when he was mortally wounded. A pal, Pte D Croft, late an employee of the Co-operative Stores, in a letter to his parents in Wright Wilson Street stated that Pte Adwick was struck in the head by shrapnel and died on his way to the dressing station. This account was different from the one given in a letter from Pte Adwick's commanding officer. In a letter to Stanley's parents he said,

" I was not actually with your son when he was killed, but I have been able to get the particulars of his death. His officer, Sergeant, Corporal and several other men were killed just about the same time as your son, and I went up to take the place of the officer and take up reinforcements. Your son was carrying the tripod mounting of the gun when a shell burst very close to him and killed him instantly, and when his comrades saw that nothing could be done for him they left him and ran for shelter from the very heavy shelling. It occurred in the darkness and when I got along the following day I realised it would be sending men to their death to try and fetch your son in, as no-one knew exactly where he was and the shelling was very, very heavy… He died painlessly and instantaneously whilst doing his duty under very heavy fire. He had only been with the company a short time, but he had proved himself thoroughly reliable and and had been made a leading gunner."

Stanley Adwick has no known grave and is commemorated on the Tyne Cot Memorial, Belgium.

LANCE CORPORAL WILLIAM BOOTH

27477 2nd Battalion Royal Warwickshire Regiment, formerly 4112 Sherwood Foresters (Notts and Derby Regiment).
Killed 9th October 1917.

William was the son of George (a railway platelayer) and Sarah Jane Booth of 1 Tenterflat Cottage, West Retford. He was twenty-one years old when he died.

William Booth has no known grave and is commemorated on the Tyne Cot Memorial, Belgium.

PRIVATE HENRY SUMMERSCALES
M2/081319 Army Service Corps, 886th Mechanical Transport Company, attached to 174th Siege Brigade, Royal Garrison Artillery.
Died 11th October 1917.

Harry Summerscales's parents, William and Elizabeth, lived in Shawcross, Dewsbury, Yorkshire. The 1901 Census shows Harry to be working as a farm labourer whilst his father worked as a coal hewer. At some stage Harry came to Retford and married Rose Makings in 1911. They lived at 17 Savile Street, Retford.

Harry, aged thirty-two, died of wounds on 11th October 1917 in the 61st Casualty Clearing Station, which was based at Dozinghem in Belgium.

Henry Summerscales is buried in Dozinghem Military Cemetery, Belgium.

PRIVATE CHARLES BRAMMER
53299 11th Battalion Sherwood Foresters (Notts and Derby Regiment).
Killed 17th October 1917.

Charles Brammer was thirty-seven years of age when he was killed. He was married to Edith E., of 16 St. John Street, Retford. He was the son of Mr. and Mrs. Charles Brammer, of Woolpack Street, Retford. The report of his death in the Retford Times was under the heading "Too Old For Trench Life", and had an extract of a letter from the CO of his Company stating: "He was such a nice and good man and such a trustworthy fellow, but he really was too old to have to go through the trials of trench life". He left a widow and five children. Prior to enlisting in June 1916 at thirty-seven years of age, Charles worked for Mr H Fletcher at Forest Farm.

Charles Brammer has no known grave and is commemorated on Tyne Cot Memorial, Belgium.

PRIVATE JOHN PERONN
59928 15th Sherwood Foresters (Notts and Derby Regiment).
Killed 22nd October 1917

John Perron was from a well-known Retford family and his sister, Mrs Robinson, lived in Savile Street. John attended the Wesleyan School. The 1911 Census shows him, employed as a printer's compositor, living at 20 Hatfield Street, Retford with his wife , Edith, who he'd married in about 1905.

He enlisted in Ilkeston and was thirty-six years of age when he died. The Commonwealth War Graves Commission shows Edith Perron living at 16 Beardsall Row.

The 15th Sherwood Foresters were originally a Bantam Battalion, made up of soldiers who were under the normal regulation minimum height of 5 feet 3 inches (1.6m). By the end of 1916 the standard of fitness of new recruits was falling well below the standard required and thereafter no more men were admitted below regulation height.

Extract from The Diary of the 15th Sherwoods, October 1917.

1st : Moved by motor transport to Peronne. Stayed until 3rd.

3rd : Entrained at midnight for XVII Corps area, and detrained at Arras at 4.30am on 4th, moving into billets at Warlus. Reorganised and rested here for several days.

13th : Entrained at Arras station at 12.54 pm, detraining at Cassel at 8.30 pm and into billets at Arneke.

15th : Entrained at Arneke at noon, detraining at Proven at 2.30pm and moved into D4 Camp.

16th : Entrained at Proven at noon, detrained at Elverdinge. Relieved the 1st Scots Guards in Rugby Camp. Battalion transport near Woesten. Whilst a Rugby Camp provided working parties for preparing new forward gun positions. Officers carried out reconnaissance of positions south of Houthulst Forest.

20th : 5pm moved to Gouvy Farm near Boesinghe.

21st : Moved to assembly positions as support to 105 Brigade, who are to be part of a general attack on 22nd.

22nd : [The day John Peronn was killed]. Operations south of Houthulst. Casualties: Officers 1 killed, 1 wounded and 1 missing; Other Ranks 15 killed, 160 missing and 20 missing.

30th : 4am. Very heavy artillery fire on ground immediately behind our front line. 6am Our snipers hit several enemy seen running about in the wood east of Marechal House. Our casualties today: 1 officer and 4 OR killed, 1 officer and 14 OR wounded.

31st : Quiet with occasional bursts of shellfire on Battalion HQ. From 4.30pm, the enemy sent over constant streams of gas shells on our back areas.

John Peronn is buried in Artillery Wood Cemetery, near Boezinge, Belgium.

Private John Perron's grave in Artillery Wood Cemetery

GUNNER WILLIAM HENRY COLLINGBURN
34839 Royal Field Artillery 'A' Battery 95th Brigade.
Died 31st October 1917.

Although William was listed as having died on 31st October 1917, Mr and Mrs Herbert Collingburn, his parents, of 37 London Road, Retford, were not informed until 13th November 1917.

Gunner Collingburn died of the effects of gas in a Canadian Clearing station near Lijssenthoek. Although only nineteen years and seven months when he died, William had seen a great deal of fighting, having enlisted in September 1914 as a sixteen-year-old. The report in the Retford Times stated that William had had a bright future before him. He had gained a scholarship at Easingwold Grammar School from Brafferton National School in North Yorkshire. William Henry Collingburn was born in Helperby, Yorks.

A letter from William's commanding officer, Captain White, was published in the Retford Times. The letter said: "It is with the very deepest regret that I learnt of the death of your son, Gunner W. Collingburn, who was admitted to the Casualty Clearing Station on October 30th (1917) suffering from gas shell poisoning. His death is a very sad loss to me. He was a splendid gunner, absolutely without fear, and always so polite and cheerful under the circumstances... His unfortunate death is a loss to us all. Please accept my sincere sympathies and those of the other officers in your sad bereavement."

William Collingburn is buried at Lijssenthoek Military Cemetery, Belgium.

LIEUTENANT HUBERT WILLIAM RAYNER
10th (Service) Battalion Royal Welsh Fusiliers attached to the 76th Trench Mortar Battery.
Died 5th November 1917.

Hubert was the son of Joseph Rayner, a former Postmaster of Retford and was educated at Retford Grammar School. Hubert died from gas poisoning. A gas shell hit the entrance to the dug-out while he was sleeping inside. He woke suffering distress from the poison fumes, and walked to the Field Dressing Station. He was moved to the Field Ambulance where he died the same evening. The day before this happened he had written to his parents a most cheerful and happy letter. The testimony of his comrades is that he was "one of the best loved and respected by all; one who by his example inspired all men under him".

Hubert Rayner is buried in Favreuil British Cemetery, France.

LANCE CORPORAL ROBERT COLTON GAGG
1st/1st Lincolnshire Yeomanry.
Died 18 November 1917.

Lance Corporal Robert Colton Gagg was born in Retford, and his father was a lock-keeper living at Lock House, Retford. Robert at some stage moved to Lincoln and married Ida. Robert, whilst living in Lincoln, was employed by the General Post Office and was also a member of the Lincolnshire Yeomanry. On 4th August 1914 Robert joined his regiment at Louth following mobilisation. The Brigade that the Lincs Yeomanry were attached to received orders to move to Salonika. These orders were changed and the Brigade headed for Egypt. The Lincs Yeomanry were on the SS Mercian in the Mediterranean when it was attacked by a surfaced U-boat. A fire- fight followed; with the men using their weapons against the submarine. The running fight lasted until the Mercian reached the North African coast, during which Robert Gagg was wounded.

The Lincolnshire Yeomanry War Diary states:

"About 100 men and horses had been killed or wounded. The dead were buried at sea the next morning. We were lucky in having our own MO., Major Purves, aboard as he attended to our many wounded until we reached Oran in North Africa and then supervised their treatment in the French Foreign Legion hospital there. As soon as the worst holes in the Mercian's plating had been patched up and the "walking wounded" were fit to travel we set forth on our journey again and arrived at Malta. Here there were more repairs, and a 12 pounder naval gun was fixed on the stern-house. Two enormous Marines came aboard as our gun-crew."

Robert Gagg is buried at Deir al-Balah Cemetery in Palestine.

PRIVATE JAMES PETTINGER
76245 1st Sherwood Foresters (Notts and Derby Regiment).
Killed on 21st November 1917.

James Pettinger was amongst the last casualties at the end of the Third Battle of Ypres. Having taken part in the opening action of this major battle on 31st July 1917, the 1st Battalion spent August, September and October moving to various places in and around the Ypres area, providing support and working parties, including spending time with the 2nd Australian Corps helping to construct a light railway. Casualties were still suffered, as even in support the Battalion faced regular shelling.

November started with the Battalion in the front line. On 17th November the Battalion was moved up through Brandhoek and Wieltje and on in to the front line north of Passchendaele. It was whilst holding this line that Pte James Pettinger was killed as the Battalion was subject to heavy artillery fire. Three days after James's death the Battalion moved back into divisional support.

James Pettinger is buried in Passchendaele New British Cemetery, Belgium.

LANCE CORPORAL JIM PALETHORPE
26477 2nd/5th Duke of Wellington's (West Riding Regiment).
Killed 27th November 1917.

The Retford Times of the 18th January 1918 wrote: "Mr and Mrs Palethorpe, late of 49 Darrel Road, Retford, have received news that their son, Lance Corporal Jim Palethorpe, is missing since 27th November 1917.

He belonged to the West Riding (Duke of Wellington's Regiment) and went to France on June 16th 1916. Previous to leaving Retford he was employed at the Northern Rubber Works.

He was also a member of the Primitive Methodist Sunday School and was educated at the St Saviour's School. He was 21 years of age".

Jim Palethorpe has no known grave and is commemorated on the Cambrai Memorial, Louverval, France.

PRIVATE THOMAS NEVILLE LISTER
275887 Nottinghamshire Yeomanry (Sherwood Rangers).
Died 29th November 1917l

Thomas Lister was the son of Thomas and Mary Lister who resided at 2 Victoria Road, Retford at the time of Thomas's death, his father was a solicitor's clerk.

Thomas was in the Sherwood Rangers, and had seen action in Salonika. He returned to Egypt in June 1917 where his unit formed part of the Desert Mounted Corps.

Pte Lister died, aged twenty-one, possibly from wounds sustained in the Battle of Nabi Samwil (20th to 24th November 1917) or in a follow-up action.

Thomas Lister has no known grave and is commemorated on the Jerusalem Memorial, Israel.

SECOND LIEUTENANT JOHN HENRY ROBINSON
4th Battalion Somerset Light Infantry, attached to 2nd/6th Battalion North Staffordshire Regiment..
Killed November 30th 1917

John Henry Robinson was the son of Mr. J H. Robinson, who was a well-known and "highly respected" Retford solicitor, and Augusta J Robinson. At the time of the census John, aged seven, lived at 119 Queens Street, Retford, with his mother and an older sister, Beatrice, aged thirteen.

John attended Retford Grammar School from 1898 to 1906. This period was followed by a brief spell at Nottingham High School.

He entered Queen's College, Cambridge and graduated with a BA in 1910 and an MA in 1914. Following his success at university, he was articled to Mr S H Clay, a Retford Solicitor.

On passing his final Law Examination he joined S H Clay, with whom he subsequently entered into partnership. This all-too-brief partnership was interrupted by the outbreak of war, when John Henry Robinson became one of the first to volunteer for service, making several attempts to join one of the Public Schools Battalions, Royal Fusiliers, only to be turned down due to an eyesight problem.

He eventually joined the Sherwood Ranger Yeo¬manry as a trooper, being swiftly promoted to Lance Corporal, and was engaged as a motorcycle dispatch rider. In 1916 he joined an Officer Cadet Battalion and found himself based in Newmarket, whence he was gazetted to a commission in the 4th Battalion Somerset Light Infantry and was stationed at Bournemouth, as Lieutenant. He was sent to the Front almost at once, being attached to the North Staffordshire Regiment with which he saw a good deal of fighting in France. He was killed on 30th November 1917 at the front near Cambrai.

John Robinson has no known grave and is commemorated on the Cambrai Memorial, France.

GEORGE WILLIAM HOUGHTON (SPELT HAUGHTON ON THE MEMORIAL)
116th Company Machine Gun Corps (Infantry), formerly 15045 Sherwood Foresters (Notts and Derby Regiment).
Died 10th December 1917.

George Houghton was the son of Mrs E Houghton of 57 Moorgate, Retford. According to records, George William Houghton was born in Sheffield, but the family moved to Retford, where George enlisted, originally with the Notts and Derbys.

George Houghton is buried in Adinkerke Military Cemetery, Belgium.

1918

GUNNER TREVOR JOHN HOLLIDAY

140562 'D' Battery 261st Brigade Royal Field Artillery.
Died 21st February 1918.

The Retford Times of 22nd March 1918 brought the news that Gunner Trevor John Holliday, Royal Field Artillery (RFA), had made the great sacrifice. Gunner Holliday was serving with 'D' Battery of the 261st Brigade RFA. He was killed in action in France on 21st February 1918, along with his officer. Prior to joining the army in April 1916, he was employed at Boots Cash Chemist and the Nelson Meat Shop and lived at No 7 Protestant Place, Queen Street, Retford. He was twenty-seven years of age and married to Clara; they had a little girl. At the time of his death Gunner Holliday had three brothers serving: Sergeant W Holliday in the Royal Garrison Artillery, who was based in Salonika; Pte Walter Holliday with the Sherwood Foresters in France; and Pte James Holliday of the Highland Light Infantry, who was wounded in France, eventually returning to his unit. Their parents were Mrs and Mrs C Holliday of Betson's Wharf, Retford.

Trevor Holliday is buried in Roclincourt Military Cemetery, France.

CORPORAL HERBERT VALLANCE

22678 7th Battalion Lincolnshire Regiment.
Killed 8th March 1918.

In the same Retford Times edition which announced the death of Trevor Holliday came the announcement of the death of Herbert Vallance. Herbert's mother lived in Garnett's Yard, Bridgegate. The report stated that his mother had received information that her son, Corporal Herbert Vallance, Lincs. Regiment, had been killed in France on 8th March 1918. He was twenty-three years of age. Prior to enlisting, Herbert worked in farm service with Mr Selby of Saundby Park. The article stated that Herbert "has seen two and a half years' service and had taken part in some hard fighting". Another son, Pte Sam Vallance, had been killed in France on 15th September 1916.

Mrs Vallance had five other sons serving: Pte W Johnson Vallance, who served in France with the Sherwood Foresters, and was twice wounded; Pte John Vallance, Leicestershire Regiment, who served in Mesopotamia and Egypt and also was wounded; Pte Ernest Vallance, Sherwood Foresters, who served in Egypt and was also wounded; Pte Albert Vallance, who served with the Royal Army Medical Corps (RAMC) in Italy; and Pte Bert Vallance, who served with the RAMC in England.

The report contained an extract from Herbert's Company Captain stating that " Nothing I can say I am afraid will appease your sorrow for the loss of your brave boy, but it will, I am sure, be some consolation to you to know that he met his death gallantly with his face towards the enemy. We all feel his death keenly, as he was always a cheerful and trustworthy NCO, and one of the most capable in his company."

The History of the Lincolnshire Regiment in the Great War tells us that from 1st January 1918 to the third week in March the 7th Battalion (51st Brigade, 17th Division) held front-line trenches around Flesquieres (southwest of Cambrai), where some of the heaviest fighting took place. It was during these actions that Herbert Vallance lost his life.

Herbert Vallance is buried in Flesquieres Hill British Cemetery, France.

LANCE CORPORAL RICHARD ROSSINGTON
305312 2nd Sherwood Foresters (Notts and Derby Regiment).
Died 14th March 1918.

Lance Corporal Richard Rossington was the son of John and Lucy Rossington, of Spring Gardens, Retford.

His death was reported on 14th March 1918. Lance Corporal Rossington had succumbed to the wounds to the hand and chest that he had received in battle the previous day.

Pte Rossington had only just returned to France from leave on 5th March 1918. He had previously been wounded on five other occasions. The Rossington family had already lost another son, Pte John Rossington, who was serving with the 1/8th Sherwood Foresters when he was killed in July 1915.

Two other sons, Corporal William Rossington and Company Sergeant Major Thomas Rossington, survived the war.

On the anniversary of his death the family placed this poem in the In Memoriam section of the Retford Times:

He sleeps not in his native land
But 'neath a foreign sky
Far from those who loved him best,
But in a hero's grave he lies.
And thus he went, a noble lad
Prepared to pay the price
To shield his home and those he loved:
A noble sacrifice.

From his sorrowing mother, father, brothers and sisters

Richard Rossington is buried in Achiet-le-Grand Communal Cemetery Extension, France.

PRIVATE PERCY CLEMENTS
53105 9th Battalion West Yorkshire Regiment (Prince of Wales's Own).
Died 16th March 1918.

Percy was reported in the Retford Times in June 1918 as having died of wounds. He actually died on 16th March 1918. He was aged nineteen, the youngest son of George and Elizabeth Clements of 7 Century Road, Retford.

Percy Clements is buried in Lapugnoy Military Cemetery, France.

Private Leslie Leonard Dixon 1729 1st Battalion Lincolnshire Regiment.
Killed 21st March 1918.

21st March 1918 saw the start of the great German Offensive known as Kaiserschlact (Kaiser Battle). This massive offensive was split into four different operations: Michael, Georgette, Gneisenau and Blucher-Yorck. It was during Operation Michael that Pte Leslie Dixon was killed. Following a four-hour bombardment starting at 5.00am, the Germans advanced on the 21st Division, of which the 1st Lincolns were part, in and around the Epehy sector. The morning was very foggy and the 1st Lincolns reported that the Germans had broken through at 10.00am. The Battalion fell back to Genin Well Copse, forming a defensive line. The Battalion were relieved on 22nd March 1918 by the South African Scottish; by this time the Battalion had had a number of casualties, including Leslie Dixon.

Leslie Dixon has no known grave and is commemorated on the Poizieres Memorial, France

LANCE SERGEANT GEORGE GILL
204815 2nd/7th Sherwood Foresters (Notts and Derby Regiment).
Killed 21st March 1918.

Notification that Sergeant George Gill was missing did not reach Retford until late April when Mrs Gill (formerly Holliday) of Grove received official information of his plight. Although posted missing, information from his fighting colleagues proved correct. One such letter said that they had seen George "in some difficulty and feared he had been killed". George, who joined the Sherwood Rangers in 1914, later to be transferred to the Sherwood Foresters, was well known as a footballer in the team playing for the town club. Before enlisting, George was a pattern- maker at Messrs Jenkins and Co. He had a brother, Frank, who, when serving with the Leicester Regiment, was taken prisoner in 1917.

George Gill has no known grave and his name is commemorated on the Arras Memorial, France.

PRIVATE JOSEPH REGINALD CUTLER
90732 2/5th Sherwood Foresters (Notts and Derby Regiment).
Killed 21st March 1918.

According to records, Joseph Cutler was born in Stamford, Lincolnshire, but enlisted in the army in Retford. The 1901 They were living in Ordsall, where Joseph (Snr) was described as employed as a painter and decorator. Records show that brother Charles enlisted in the Lincolnshire Regiment and survived the war.

Joseph Cutler has no known grave and is commemorated on the Arras Memorial, France.

PRIVATE JOHN WILLIAM ALLISON
97879 1st Battalion Sherwood Foresters (Notts and Derby Regiment).
Killed 26th March 1918.

John William Allison was born in Woodhouse, near Sheffield. In 1911, aged twelve, he was living at 18 Trent Trent Street, Retford with his parents and three siblings. His father was a railway signalman. He enlisted in Doncaster according to Soldiers Died in the Great War.

John Allison has no known grave and is commemorated on the Poizieres Memorial, France.

LANCE SERGEANT FRANK SNOWDIN DCM

4086116th Battalion Manchester Regiment, formerly 4045 2nd/8th Sherwood Foresters (Notts and Derby Regiment).
Killed 23rd March 1918.

The announcement of Frank Snowdin's award of the DCM was made on 24th January 1917 in the London Gazette. This prompted the following report in the Retford Times dated 2nd February 1917:

"We published in our last issue a further list of honours and promotions from Wednesday's 'London Gazette' and amongst the Notts and Derbys men who had been awarded the Distinguished Conduct Medal was Private Frank Snowdin. We have since learned that Private Snowdin is a Retford man and is the second son of Mr and Mrs Harry Snowdin, 87 Moorgate. As a boy he attended St Saviour's School and after leaving there was employed for three years by Mr R Gibson, Keeper of the Municipal Buildings. Then he went to the Northern Rubber Works and in June 1915 joined the 2/8th Sherwood Foresters. He underwent his training in Watford and Dunstable, and served in the Irish Rebellion, where he was wounded twice in the leg.

Pte Snowdin was one of a number who distinguished themselves and received congratulations form Lieut Colonel W Coape Oates, commanding the Battalion, for gallantry and coolness in the field. He went with a draft of men last September (1916) from Ireland to France and was transferred to the Manchester Regiment. His mother received a letter from him last Friday. He was at the time of writing out of the trenches, enjoying a five-week rest. He had fought in the Battle of the Somme. He has not been home since last March (1916). Pte Snowdin is 19 years of age and his distinction reflects the honour upon his native town. His parents have not yet received information on how their son gained the honour."

Frank Snowdin has no known grave and is commemorated on the Pozieres Memorial, France.

LANCE SERGEANT FRED JOHN STOCKDALE MM

12353 2nd Battalion Grenadier Guards.
Killed 28th March 1918.

Mr and Mrs Stockdale of Beech Cottage, Ordsall, received a letter saying that their second son Sergeant F J Stockdale, Grenadier Guards, had been killed in action in France on 28th March. The chaplain, in his letter, described how bravely and nobly he died and mentioned that he was buried where he fell.

The deceased was thirty-four years of age and as a boy was a member of the Ordsall Church choir and attended Thrumpton Lane School. He was a groom at the West Retford Hall, had joined the Sherwood Ranger Yeomanry. He had previously volunteered for service in the South African War. In 1914 he joined the regular army and had fought for his country since the beginning of the war.

He had recently won the Military Medal and had been mentioned in dispatches. He had been home on leave three times, the last being in October 1917. A brother, Reginald Stockdale, Sherwood Foresters, was also in France.

Fred Stockdale is buried at Bucquoy Road Cemetery, Ficheux, France.

PRIVATE CHARLES TALBOT

90733 1st/5th Sherwood Foresters (Notts and Derby Regiment).
Killed 1st April 1918.

Charles Talbot was just twenty years old when he was killed in France on 1st April 1918. He was the youngest son of Mr and Mrs Charles Talbot of Cottam. Before joining the Sherwood Foresters in July 1917 Charles was employed in the Loco Department of the Great Central railways in Retford. He lived with his sister, Mrs Snowden of Humber Street, whose husband also saw action in the war, serving with the Durham Light Infantry.

Charles Talbot is buried in Aix-Noulette Communal Cemetery Extension

PRIVATE THOMAS HENRY MARSH

94294 12th Battalion Sherwood Foresters (Notts and Derby Regiment).
Died 9th April 1918.

The news was reported in the Retford Times that Private T H Marsh, who lived at 19 Poplar Street, Retford, son of Mr and Mrs J Marsh, Ladybridge Cottages, Babworth, died of wounds on 9th April at No 8 Stationary Hospital, France (Wimereux).

The deceased was employed on the Babworth Estate under Brigadier General Davison before joining the army; his father had worked on the Babworth Estate for some forty years.

He joined up on 23rd January 1916 but was sent home. He was called up again on 20th February 1917 and was wounded on 29th March 1917. He left a widow and two children. He was forty years of age.

Thomas Marsh is buried at Wimereux Communal Cemetery, France.

PRIVATE CHARLES OSTICK

260112 2nd/5th Hampshire Regiment, formerly 3460 Sherwood Foresters (Notts and Derby Regiment).
Killed 10th April1918.

Charles Ostick, son of Albert and Mary Ostick of Moorgate was serving with the 2/5th Hampshires in Palestine when he was killed by a grenade whilst on a raid. Charles had served with the Notts and Derbys prior to his transfer to the Hampshires.

Charles Ostick is buried in the Ramleh War Cemetery, Israel

PRIVATE JOHN HERBERT SHAW

64527 15th Battalion Sherwood Foresters (Notts and Derby Regiment) attached to the 105th Trench Mortar Battery.
Killed 10th April 1918.,

Shaw enlisted in the 15th Sherwood Foresters, but at the time of his death he was attached to the 105th Trench Mortar Battery. Captain Wotton of the Trench Mortar Battery wrote: "Whilst carrying ammunition to the front line a shell landed amongst our men and killed several, including your husband. Death in every case was instantaneous. Your husband had only been with this unit since February, but he had shown himself to be a willing and hardworking soldier."

John was married to Ethel and they lived at 12 Wharf Road, Retford. He was thirty-four years old when he was killed. He had attended the Wesleyan School and on leaving found an apprenticeship, as a butcher, with George Tallents, being later employed by Mr Farrington of Carolgate. His death left a widow and six children, the eldest being twelve years of age. He had enlisted in 1916 and was trained at Sunderland, embarking for France on 1st February 1917.

Having been wounded on 31st July 1917 (possibly at Passchendaele), he spent time at Southwark Military Hospital, returning to his unit on 31st October 1917. John had two other brothers serving in the forces: the younger brother, Jarvis, served in France, Egypt, Salonika and the Dardanelles; the older brother, Charles, served with Royal Field Artillery, Transport Section.

John Shaw has no known grave and is commemorated on Poizieres Memorial, France.

PRIVATE JOHN (JACK) DODSON

242111 8th Battalion Border Regiment, formerly 51628 Sherwood Foresters (Notts and Derby Regiment), 4229 Duke of Wellington's (West Riding) Regiment and 4569 Border Regiment..
Died 11th April 1918.

Following the Armistice in November 1918, more news came out about soldiers reported missing and prisoners of war. One such case was the confirmation of the death of Pte Jack Dodson. Jack Dodson went missing in April 1918 and was reported as a prisoner of war. In fact, Pte Dodson died from serious stomach wounds whilst a prisoner of war

Jack, known locally as a good footballer and cricketer, joined the colours in 1916. Following three months training at Brocton camp in Staffordshire, Jack was drafted into the 8th Battalion Border Regiment, having served with the Sherwood Foresters and West Riding Regiment. As a marksman and a Lewis Gunner Jack would have been involved in some tough action. It was following a period of leave that Jack returned to France on Easter Sunday 1918; ten days later he was reported missing.

Jack Dodson was the son of Mr and Mrs Fred Dodson, who lived in Keyworth, near Nottingham. Jack was married to Gertrude, who at the time of his death was living with her parents at 5 Wright Wilson Street. It was at this address that she received Jack's wallet from a fellow prisoner, who said that he "was badly wounded in the abdomen and that he had requested that the wallet should be forwarded to his wife".

Jack Dodson is buried in Tourcoing (Pont-Neuville) Communal Cemetery, France.

LANCE CORPORAL HENRY SWANNACK

365882 A Company 1st/4th Battalion Northumberland Fusiliers.
Died 11th April 1918.

The Retford Times reported:
"On Saturday morning Alderman and Mrs Swannack, Grove Street, Retford, received news that their son, Lance Corporal Henry Swannack, Northumberland Fusiliers, had died in 33rd Casualty Clearing Station at Haverskerque, from shell wounds received on 11th April 1918.

Henry had been employed in the family's furniture business. He had married Ethel Robertson, who had been a journalist with the Retford Times, in 1915; they had one child, who had been christened a month prior to Henry's death. Henry had three other brothers who served: Private Arthur Swannack, Lieutenant Fred Swannack and

Corporal Clement Swannack, who was medically discharged having served in France.

Henry Swannack is buried in Haverskerque British Cemetery, France.

PRIVATE JOSEPH DIXON
42026 4th Battalion South Staffordshire Regiment.
Died 10th April 1918.

Joseph Dixon (Joe) was born in early 1881; the Census records of that year show him as being two months old. Joe, as he was known, was born in Eaton, just outside Retford, where his father, Henry, was employed as a farm servant. Henry was twenty-four at that time and was married to Emma (twenty-two). The Census shows that they already had another son, William, aged two. Joe's father's birthplace is shown as Langwith whilst his mother originated from Retford.

Joe enlisted in the South Staffs 4th (Extra Reserve) Battalion, which had been stationed in Lichfield, embarking for France in October 1917, attached to the 7th Brigade, 25th Division. Joe's father, living at Thrumpton Lane, received news in June that his son was missing after being involved in action. The Retford Times of 7th June 1918 reported that, having gone to France in October 1917, he "saw a lot of hard fighting." This would have been at Passchendaele, where the 7th Division were in action. He was one of the first in Retford to enlist under Lord Derby's scheme, but was not liberated from service with the Great Northern Railway Company until June 1917. He was a fitter's labourer and formerly a verger at St Alban's Church. He was a single man of thirty-seven.

Joseph Dixon is buried in Harlebeke New British Cemetery, Belgium.

PRIVATE WALTER BELL
19829 4th Battalion The King's (Liverpool Regiment).
Died 11th April 1918.

Walter had enlisted early in 1917 in Sheffield. News of his death reached Retford on 18th May 1918. He is buried in Chocques Military Cemetery in a large collective grave which contains the remains of twenty-eight other soldiers of the 4th King's Liverpool Regiment, who were killed in a troop train that had been shelled in April 1918. Pte Bell died of wounds received in this incident. Walter Bell was the brother of Mrs Wilkinson and Mrs Goy, both of Ordsall.

Walter Bell is buried in Chocques Military Cemetery, France.

PRIVATE HORACE EDGAR HIGGS

2033871st/4th Battalion York and Lancaster Regiment.
Killed 12th April 1918;

Horace was the son of Francis Richard Higgs, a railway signalman, and his wife, Hannah, of Swiss Cottage, Babworth Park, Retford. He was the husband of Maggie Higgs, who he had married in 1910, of 74 Mona Road, Sheffield. They had a daughter, Margaret. Horace was thirty-three years of age when he was killed. The 1911 Census shows him as a sorting clerk and telegraphist with the Post Office.

Horace Higgs has no known grave and is commemorated on the Tyne Cot Memorial, Belgium.

PRIVATE REGINALD HAROLD WOOD

275341 3rd (City of London) Battalion (Royal Fusiliers) attached to the 2nd Battalion Royal Fusiliers, formerly 2675 East Kent Regiment.
Died 13th April 1918.

Reginald Wood was the son of Mr. Alfred Owen Wood, who was Stationmaster at Retford and lived at Fletton House (near to the station). Reginald had previously been badly wounded in the head by shrapnel, recovered and rejoined his unit. He was posted as "missing" between 11th and 13th April 1918.

Reginald Wood has no known grave and his name is commemorated on the Ploegsteert Memorial, Belgium.

LANCE SERGEANT FRED HARRISON

235371 2nd/4th Battalion Leicestershire Regiment, formerly 2232 Nottinghamshire Yeomanry (Sherwood Rangers) and Sherwood Foresters (Notts and Derby Regiment). Killed 16th April 1918.

Fred Harrison enlisted with the Sherwood Rangers in November 1914. His training with the regiment took place in Norfolk, Essex and Kent. Following his training, Fred qualified as an instructor and gained his First Class Certificate in Musketry. Early in 1918 he, with others, was transferred to the Sherwood Foresters, and upon arriving in France in February 1918, to the Leicesters.

In a letter to the Retford Times, Sergeant C M Chapman, also of the Leicesters, stated that "we were in reserve line, when we were heavily shelled. Poor Fred and four others stood no chance with one that almost dropped on top of him. Death was instantaneous and they suffered no pain. You can understand what a shock it was to myself and Sergeant Hill when we heard such news, for we three have been great pals ever since the Second Battalion Sherwood Rangers was formed at Retford. We feel his loss like that of a brother and the lads that came out with our draft all feel his death very much. We can assure you that he was greatly respected by all the boys. We did not see him buried but found his grave close to the spot where he was killed. There was a cross erected upon it". Sergeant Chapman was probably trying to lessen the sorrow with the last statement.

He was the son of Mr Thomas Harrison, Clinton Terrace, Retford, and after leaving the Council School was employed at the Beehive Works. He was a well-known Retford Football Club player and the holder of a medal won in 1917 in connection with his Brigade. His wife was the daughter of Mr John Bellamy, West Markham. She and her three children lived at 4 Whitehall Road, Retford.

Fred Harrison has no known grave and is commemorated on the Ploegsteert Memorial, Belgium.

GUNNER ROBERT SLY

129313 'A' Battery 52nd Brigade Royal Field Artillery.
Killed 22nd April 1918.

Robert Sly was the youngest son of Mr and Mrs Sly of Retford. Robert's mother's origins were in Horncastle, Lincolnshire. Prior to his enlistment, Robert worked in Doncaster for Great Northern Railways in the Signalling Department.

Although Robert was killed on 21st April 1 1918, official news of his death did not reach Retford until early June 1918. He had joined the army at the age of seventeen and embarked for France when he was eighteen, following periods of training in Newcastle. Having reached France, he was then sent to Ireland. On his way for a period of leave the transporter he was sailing on was hit by a trawler; he was rescued by a destroyer but unfortunately lost all of his possessions. Following this period of leave, he again was sent to France where he had been only a fortnight when he was killed, aged nineteen.

Robert Sly is buried in La Targette British Cemetery, Neuville-St Vaast, France.

PRIVATE ALFRED HEMPSALL
268005 2nd/7th Battalion Sherwood Foresters (Notts and Derby Regiment).
Killed 26th April 1918.

Alfred was the son of William and Elizabeth Hempsall of 94 Thrumpton Lane. The 1911 Census shows him employed as a railway lampman.

Alfred Hempsall is buried in Mons (Bergen) Communal Cemetery, Belgium.

PRIVATE WILLIAM MEAD
235488 6th Battalion Leicestershire Regiment.
Killed 29th April 1918.

The circumstances of William's death were explained in the course of a letter written by Lance Corporal Gleaden (to die as Sergeant Gleaden MM later in 1918) to his wife:

"We were in a hot corner under a heavy barrage and a shell fell where we were taking shelter. Poor Mead was killed instantaneously and Beardsall was so severely wounded that he died two days later [see below]. I was terribly upset when I heard about it next morning. They were such promising young men and Beardsall was in for a promotion. They were chums to be proud of and were most devoted to each other. I had the highest respect and esteem for both of them. We had often spoken of the happy times we would spend together if we had the luck to pull through. Mead was one of the squarest of men I have met, and tried to do his best for all. Please convey my deepest sympathy to Mrs Mead and Mrs Beardsall".

It appears that Lance Corporal Gleaden and Ptes Mead and Beardsall had served three years in the Sherwood Foresters. They had all been wounded and returned together to France on Easter Sunday. It was then that they were transferred to the Leicesters.

The late Pte Mead was a native of Whitby and had lived in Retford for seven years. He was employed by the Retford Co-operative Society and by Wright Bros. He was thirty years of age, married to Jenny, who lived at 2 Tiln Road, and left two children. Two of his brothers had been discharged from the army having been incapacitated. Mrs Mead was the sister of Mrs S Needham, Biggins Cottage, Babworth.

William Mead is buried in the Divisional Collecting Cemetery and Extension, Ypres.

PRIVATE WILLIAM BEARDSALL MM
235517 6th Battalion Leicestershire Regiment, formerly 306188 Sherwood Foresters (Notts and Derby Regiment).
Died 3rd May 1918.

The 1901 Census shows William living with his mother, Clara and his father John at 3 Wellington Street, Retford. As well as William (aged fifteen) the Census shows two other sons, Harold and John.

A Citation from Housley's British Gallantry Awards - The Sherwood Foresters reads:

'For conspicuous gallantry and devotion to duty, during the attack at St Julien between 26th and 28th September 1917. When all the Officers and NCO's of the platoon had become casualties, Private Beardsall with splendid initiative took command of his platoon and led them forward to their objective.'

It was for this action that William was awarded the Military Medal.

In a report dated 8th February 1918, it stated that William Beardsall had been wounded and gassed and was due to return to France from his hospitalisation in Ripon, having previously received treatment in Derbyshire. This may well have been the point at which William was transferred to the Leicesters. It is also noted that William had served during the Irish Rebellion and had "come through unscathed."

In a report headlined "Retford Military Medallist", The Retford Times of the 7th June 1918 reported:

"Mrs Beardsall of 49, West Street, Retford, received official information of the death of her husband, Private William Beardsall, Sherwood Foresters. In June 1918 the widow received two very sympathetic letters from the Matron of the hospital where he died in France in which she stated he was wounded in the head on May 1st when coming out of the trenches and died on May 3rd. In March 1918 Pte Beardsall was presented by the Mayor of Retford with the Military Medal for bravery in the field and at the time of his death was about to receive a promotion. He was the son of Mr and Mrs John Beardsall, Churchgate, Retford, and prior to joining the war worked at Manton Pit and lived in Worksop. The widow Mrs Beardsall had a brother, Pte J Padley in the ASC Motor Transports. Trooper Jack Beardsall was in the Royal Horse Guards and eventually attached to the Grenadier Guards. He volunteered for service with the Household Battalion, serving in France. He spent some time in hospital in Eastbourne with trench feet and sceptic poisoning. Pte Beardsall was a member of the Retford Volunteer Corps before he transferred to the Territorials".

William Beardsall is buried in the Etaples Military Cemetery, France.

PRIVATE GEORGE WILLIAM ALLEN
83381 1st Battalion Sherwood Foresters (Notts and Derby Regiment).
Killed 27th May 1918.

Married to Mary and the father to two daughters, Winifred and Roxana, George Allen had recently established a butcher's shop on Woolpack Street when war was declared. In 1916, his family was living on Trent Street when a Zeppelin dropped bombs on Retford, and 6 year old Roxana was injured by a large fragment of glass which embedded in her knee. Shortly afterwards George came home on embarkation leave, the last time the family saw him alive, except for a fleeting sight of him on a newsreel at the Picture Palace on Carolgate.

George was killed at the Battle of the Aisne, aged thirty-eight.

George Allen has no known grave and is commemorated on the Soissons Memorial, France.

PRIVATE (JAMES) ALLEN LEE
29876 "A" Company 7th/8th Battalion King's Own Scottish Borderers.
Died 30th May 1918.

Mrs Lee of 8 Frederick Street, Retford, received news in June of the death of her eldest son, Pte Allen Lee on 30th May 1918, from wounds received in his spine on 29th May 1918. Having joined on 1st March 1916, he went to France in January 1917, only to be invalided home with trench fever. He returned to active service on 21st June 1917. Before enlisting he worked for Messrs. Richmond and Son, builders. He was thirty years old.

Allen Lee is buried in the Aubigny Communal Cemetery Extension, France.

PRIVATE FRANCIS (FRANK) JAMES FLINTON

42887 2nd Battalion Lincolnshire Regiment.
Died 17th June 1918.

Francis James Flinton was born in 1899 in East Retford. Before enlisting, he lived with his mother at 9 Avenue Road, Retford. He was posted as missing on 21st March 1918 and nothing was heard from him until a letter arrived at Avenue Road from Frank stating that he was a prisoner of war held at an unknown camp in Germany. In the letter Frank went on to state that he had received a bad wound in the leg and that he was being treated well by his captors. Sadly, Mrs Flinton received notice that Frank had died from complications from his wounds in June 1918. Frank was just nineteen, and had been called up in 1917. Previously Frank was employed as an assistant at Melias Grocer Store in the Market Square in Retford. Frank's father, Thomas Flinton, had died some years earlier.

Frank Flinton is buried in Cologne Southern Cemetery, Germany.

PRIVATE ERNEST BREDDY

201277 5th Battalion Royal Scots Fusiliers.
Died 20th June 1918.

The Retford Times dated 19th July 1918 reported the death of Ernest Breddy, second son of Mrs Breddy of 66 Spital Hill. Pte Breddy was in the 5th Battalion of the Royal Scots Fusiliers. A letter from his Company Commander stated that he was killed by machine gun fire whilst standing at his post as a part of the Lewis Gun Section. The letter went on to state that "he always performed his duties cheerfully."

At the time of his death Ernest was thirty years of age and single. He had served his apprenticeship with J R Plant, Draper, in the Market Square; Ernest had lived in Grimsby and Lincoln before returning to Retford to start his own business as a travelling draper. Ernest had enlisted in Chelmsford, Essex in 1917.

Ernest Breddy is buried in La Targette British Cemetery, Neuville-St Vaast, France.

PRIVATE CYRIL IVAN SWIFT
G/96287 Middlesex Regiment posted to 7th Battalion London Regiment.
Died 8th August 1918.

The 1901 Census tells us that Cyril Ivan Swift was born in Retford; his father was John Swift of Leicester, a shopkeeper and draper. Cyril attended Retford Grammar School.

On reaching the age of eighteen he joined the Air Force as a Cadet, and trained for some time at Hastings, but although graded as A1, he failed to pass the final physical test as a Flying Officer, and was sent to a London infantry regiment. After his course of training at Blandford he left for France on July 17th, less than a month before he was killed. He was described in the Retfordian as "a boy of high principle and was greatly beloved by all who knew him".

Cyril fell in action near Albert on August 8th 1918, when nearly the whole of his unit became casualties under fierce, con¬centrated machine-gun fire.

Cyril Swift is buried in a plot containing seventy-six other soldiers who were killed in retaking the cemetery from German hands, having lost the ground to the enemy in the Spring Offensive of 1918. On 8th August the 7th attacked Malard Wood. They had 300 casualties in two days of fighting.

Cyril Swift is buried in Dive Copse British Cemetery, Sailly-le-Sec, France.

PRIVATE HARRY HASLAM
264234 116th Battalion Canadian Infantry.
Killed 27th August 1918.

Harry Haslam was born on 7th January 1884 in Retford. He emigrated to the United States of America in about 1905, living in Buffalo City, New York, where he was employed as a locomotive engineer. A report in the Retford Times with regards to his death states that "as the war progressed he became restless and before the United States got into the fight he heard the call, he saw the vision and went across the Canadian border and enlisted in the Canadian Highlanders".

His address on enlistment on 10th July 1916 was simply Fort Erie, in Ontario. His attestation papers show that his mother, Sarah Ann, lived at Woodland View, Pennington Walk, Retford. He arrived in England towards the end of 1916 to undergo training. In March 1917 he was sent to France.

An extract taken from the 116th Battalion diaries tell us that on 27th August 1918:

"Zero Hour was at 4.55 a.m., on the morning of the 27th, The objectives being Boiry-Notre Dame and Artillery Hill. "A" Company was to follow in support of the 52nd Battalion, "D" Company followed by "C" Company were to work along the sunken road between Bois Du Bert and Bois Du Bert. "D" Company, making direct for Artillery Hill and "C" Company to capture Boiry-Notre Dame. "B" Company was in reserve. Considerable opposition was encountered from machine guns, and further progress being impossible after the capture of these two woods it was found necessary to re-organize, the whole being under the command of Major Pratt, Major Sutherland having been killed by machine gun fire".

It was during this action that Harry was killed.

He is buried in Vis-en-Artois British Cemetery, Haucourt, France.

SERGEANT GEORGE COX
241298 22nd (Tyneside Scottish) Battalion Northumberland Fusiliers.
Killed 6th September 1918.

Sgt George Cox, second son of Mr And Mrs J B Cox of 7 Thomas Street, was killed on 6th September 1918 by a shot from a German sniper. George was married and lived at Clinton Terrace with his wife and child. Prior to enlisting he had been employed at the Northern Rubber Works, Retford. George enlisted in July 1916 and, following training at Strensall, Clevedon, Weston-super-Mare and Wellingborough, proceeded to France in June 1917 with the rank of Corporal. At St Quentin in August 1917 George was gassed and wounded and was sent back to England, spending time in Thorpe and Ripon hospitals. A year later, in August, George returned to France where just over a month later he was killed.

A letter sent to his home by his Company Commander said: "Sergeant Cox was signalling his position when the fatal bullet caught him. He had with great bravery and success brought his section to the advance post which they were to occupy and from which they had driven the Germans".

George, twenty-nine years of age, had been a devoted member of the Primitive Methodist Church, serving as the choir secretary.

George Cox is buried in Post Office Rifles Cemetery, Festubert, France.

SERGEANT FREDERICK (FRED) CHARLES BANNISTER

87163 22nd (Tyneside Scottish) Battalion Northumberland Fusiliers, formerly 10174 York and Lancaster Regiment.
Killed 6th September 1918.

Married to Kitty in 1915, Fred had enlisted in Pontefract, Yorkshire. His father, also called Frederick, was killed, serving with the Sherwood Foresters, a month later.

Fred Bannister has no known grave and is commemorated on the Loos Memorial, France.

SERGEANT CHARLES MARTIN CHAPMAN

1st Battalion Leicestershire Regiment, formerly 2082 Nottinghamshire Yeomanry (Sherwood Rangers).
Killed 19th September 1918

Charles was the first of two sons, of Mr and Mrs J Chapman of Babworth Lodge, Retford, killed within ten days of each other in France.

Charles was a sergeant serving with the 1st Leicesters at the time of his death on 19th September 1918. He was probably killed during the Battle of Epehy, which was a part of the larger battle for the Hindenburg Line. Sergeant Chapman was twenty-four years of age at the time of his death. The 1st Leicesters were attached to the 6th Division and part of the IX Corps of which the 1/5th Sherwood Foresters were part when his older brother, John Chapman, was killed on 29th September 1918, ten days later.

Charles Chapman is buried at Trefcon British Cemetery, Caulaincourt, France.

PRIVATE WILLIAM DAWSON

18368 2nd Battalion Royal Irish Regiment, formerly 203169 Lincolnshire Regiment and 40199 Royal Dublin Fusiliers.
Killed 27th September 1918.

William Dawson was twenty-seven years of age when he was killed on 27th September 1918, whilst serving with the Royal Irish Regiment. His records show that he enlisted originally with the Lincolnshire Regiment and had also served with the Royal Dublin Fusiliers.

William was the son of Mr and Mrs H Dawson of Worksop. He had worked at Threlfalls Maltkilns. He joined the colours on 16th April 1916, embarking for France on 12th March 1917. He was wounded on two occasions; this may explain why he served in three different Regiments, i.e. returning as a reinforcement following his recovery. Reports also tell us that he was buried for two hours following an artillery attack.

William Dawson is buried at Sucrerie British Cemetery, Graincourt-les-Havrincourt, France.

CORPORAL JOHN CHAPMAN
204796 1st/5th Sherwood Foresters (Notts and Derby) Regiment, formerly 2083 Nottinghamshire Yeomanry (Sherwood Rangers).
Killed 29th September 1918.

John was the second of two sons of Mr and Mrs J Chapman of Babworth Lodge, Retford, killed within ten days of each other in France.

John Chapman was a Corporal with the 1/5th Sherwood Foresters and was killed in the later stages of the battle for the Hindenburg Line, namely the Battle of the St Quentin Canal. John had been described a "bright cheerful young man of splendid physique and his genial manner made him very popular in the Army".

Both brothers had joined the Sherwood Rangers Yeomanry in 1914. During training John received a major setback, with an attack of pneumonia.

Having received treatment at the local Mrs Huntsman's VAD Hospital on Lime Tree Avenue, Retford, he soon returned to his unit. He was eventually transferred to the Notts and Derbys Regiment and before his death (aged twenty-six) had seen some hard fighting in France.

John Chapman is buried in Bellicourt British Cemetery, France.

STOKER 1ST CLASS JAMES BREDDY

SS/107895 Royal Navy.
Died 29th September 1918.

News reached Retford in October 1918 of the death of James Breddy, a stoker in the Royal Navy. His mother was informed that he had died whilst on board a lighter. One of his jobs would have been to light the boilers for the engine.

It was whilst doing this that the engine exploded, covering him in hot paraffin from a blow-torch he was using to light the engine.

This caught fire, causing extensive burns. Stoker Breddy was transported to a hospital ship where he received "the best possible attention and most skilful medical and nursing treatment."

Unfortunately, the injuries were so severe that he died. The Retford Times reports that he was buried in a "little English Cemetery abroad among the noble dead, who, like him, had been called to give their lives for their country". He received a full Naval Ceremony.

Please note that James is listed as J. Brady in official documents.

James Breddy is buried in East Mudros Military Cemetery, Greece.

PRIVATE ALFRED HOWLETT

57218 11th Battalion Sherwood Foresters (Notts and Derby Regiment).
Killed 5th October 1918.

Alfred Howlett was the eldest son of Mr and Mrs Alfred Howlett, who at the time of his death were living at 6 Wellington Street, Retford. Alfred Jnr, like his father, was a stoker at the Retford Corporation Gasworks before enlisting. He was transferred from the Sherwood Rangers to the Sherwood Foresters. He was a scholar at the Wesleyan Day School, Retford.

Alfred Howlett is buried in Guizancourt Farm Cemetery, Gouy, France.

PRIVATE FREDERICK BANNISTER

21589 11th Battalion Sherwood Foresters (Notts and Derby Regiment).
Killed 6th October 1918.

Frederick worked at Gilstrap Maltkilns, Thrumpton, before joining the colours in January 1915. The 1911 Census shows him, a maltster's labourer, living with his wife, Annie, and four of his children on Spital Hill, though, by the time of his death, the family was living at 7 Wellington Street. His eldest son, also named Frederick, was killed in action in September 1918.

In March 1916 he was sent to France, where he fought for seventeen months, and as a hardened soldier went with the rest of 70th Brigade, 23rd Division, to Italy. Here he was involved in more fighting, very likely being involved in the Battle of Asiago and the Battle of Vittorio Veneto. From September 1918 the 11th Sherwood were attached to 74th Brigade of the 25th Division and returned to France.

It was in France, probably at the Battle of Beaurevoir that Frederick went missing on 6th October 1918. His wife, Annie received the news later in October that he had been reported as missing, presumed dead. He was forty-two years old. His body was never recovered.

Frederick Bannister has no known grave and is commemorated on the Vis-en-Artois Memorial, France.

SERGEANT WILLIAM GLEADEN MM

235396 6th Battalion Leicestershire Regiment, formerly 6343 Sherwood Foresters (Notts and Derby Regiment).
Killed 8th October 1918.

William Gleaden was born in Babworth and enlisted in Retford. A grocery assistant, he and his wife, Fanny, lived at 38 Tiln Lane. He was thirty-three when he was killed.

William Gleaden has no known grave and is commemorated on the Vis-en-Artois Memorial, France.

PRIVATE JABEZ MOUNTAIN

156215 38th Battalion Machine Gun Corps, formerly 45087 South Staffordshire Regiment.
Killed 9th October 1918.

Jabez, formerly a resident of Old Leake in Lincolnshire, was employed as a horseman by J Curtis of Eaton. He left his employment and joined the colours on 3rd January 1917. At the time of his death he was thirty years of age, and left a wife, Margaret, and three children living at 1 Caledonian Road.

Jabez Mountain is buried in Prospect Hill Cemetery, Gouy, France.

PRIVATE HAROLD MELLOR VESSEY

34792 5th Battalion Yorkshire Regiment.
Died 13th October 1918.

Harold lived at 43 Wharton Street before enlisting. His parents were John and Sarah Vessey. Before enlisting, the twenty-year-old was employed on the relief staff of the Great Northern Railway Company, Retford. His father was employed as a guard on the Great Central Railway. After enlisting in Spring 1917, Harold was sent to France on 26th February 1918.

The Vessey family first received the bad news in July 1918 that Harold had been missing since 27th May 1918. This news came via the York Record Office. The sad news of his death reached them in early 1919. The information they received was that Harold had died of pleurisy while a prisoner of war. A fellow prisoner of war, who visited the Vesseys, said that Harold was a good companion and that they had been taken prisoner together. The companion then went on to say they were taken to Ramicourt. At this point, in early October 1918, they were separated. His fellow prisoner said that at this stage Harold was looking well, considering the conditions.

Harold was given a military funeral and is buried in Niederzwehren Cemetery, Germany.

SECOND LIEUTENANT ROBERT SYDNEY PLANT

1st/8th Battalion Sherwood Foresters (Notts and Derby Regiment).
Killed 17th October 1918.

Robert Plant was born in Retford and at the time of the 1901 Census lived with his parents John and Emily Plant at Holly Road, Retford. The records show that his father was an employer in the drapery trade. At the time of Robert's death the family had moved to 49 Dominie Cross, a house named The Hollies, opposite Retford Grammar School. As well as Robert, the Plants had a son named Charles Bailey Plant, who at the outbreak of the war lived in Toronto, Canada, where he worked as an engineer. At the onset of the war Charles enlisted and came to England in 1915 with the 19th Battalion and saw action at the Somme and Ypres before joining an Officer Cadet Battalion; he went on to fight as a 2nd Lieutenant in the Machine Gun Heavies (Tanks).

''We moved on again between 2 and 3am and without difficulty reached and formed up on our jumping off line, which had been previously taped out by the Brigade Major, Capt. Grinling, about 70 yards South of the Bohain-Vaux-Andigny Road. We had three companies in the front line, A on the right, B in the centre, and C on the left, D were in support behind C Company, was in the vicinity of Vallee Hasard Farm. All troops were in position by 3.45am. on October 17th. The frontage allotted to us was about 1200 yards. Zero was 5.20am. There was a certain amount of mist which developed into a dense fog. It is pretty safe to say that everyone was lost almost immediately. C company on the left kept going for some time alright and got some possession of some high ground. B Company in the centre went on until they were held up by unbroken wire. A Company on the right soon lost touch with B, but got on until they reached a position near the railway track. D company lost touch with everyone at first, and got completely split up. During the attack we captured something like 220 prisoners and nearly 100 machine guns, besides inflicting many other casualties. Our own losses too were heavy - the heaviest in Officers that we had experienced in the recent fighting. Besides Geary we lost 2nd Lieuts Plant and Jacques William Gladstone killed and Lieuts Toyne and Whitelegge and 2nd Lieut John H Smith wounded, whilst in other ranks we lost 25 killed or died of wounds and 54 wounded".
History of the 1/8th Sherwood Foresters.

Robert joined up on 14th September 1914 along with many school friends (including three others who were to perish in the war: David Tanner, Sidney Lidster, and Cecil Land) with the 1st/8th Sherwood Foresters.

He was incapacitated with knee trouble, and worked in the Records Office at Lichfield until he went into training for a commission with the 5th Battalion Sherwood Foresters. He went to France, rejoining the 1/8th Sherwood Foresters, and had only been out there five weeks when he met his death.

The Lieutenant Colonel commanding wrote to the young officer's father: "I ask you to accept my sincere sym¬pathy in the great loss you and all of us have sustained by the death of your son. He was slightly wounded, and was going back to the dressing station to have his wound attended to, when he was struck by a piece of shell which burst close to him, killing him instantaneously. I can only hope that it will be some small comfort to you that he died doing his duty like a brave British soldier, who never knew what fear meant. He was loved by every man in his platoon, who are grieved at the loss of their leader."

Robert Plant is buried in Fresnoy-le-Grand Communal Cemetery Extension, France.

PRIVATE JOHN THOMPSON
275435 14th Battalion (Kings) Hussars.
Died 19th October 1918.

John Thompson was the son of George and Sarah Thompson and resided at the Northern Inn, Cobwell Road.

Having been moved to Mesopotamia from Meerut in India, the Regiment took part in operations against Turkish forces. On 1st December 1915 the King's Hussars fought determinedly and fiercely at Umm-al-Tubal, using their firepower. The Regiment were also heavily involved in the taking of Baghdad, after which the chief Turkish position at Ramadi on the Euphrates was taken. After Ramadi the Regiment became involved in reconnaissance and patrolling duties until 1918, when it was attached to a column that operated inside Persia.

"Influenza had become almost an epidemic in Bijar by October 12th. There were 150 cases. First of all our Indian servants got it; we had to do everything ourselves, including cooking. The Colonel's boy and poor old Haji the interpreter got it. Then all the officers got it. The Colonel was the only one exempted. It turned to pneumonia in the severer cases. In a week, we had seven deaths of British soldiers; four were our own men, and nineteen Indians died."

Historical Record of the 14th (King's) Hussars

It is likely that John was one of those four men who died from pneumonia brought on by influenza.

John Thompson has no known grave and is commemorated on the Tehran Memorial, Iran.

PRIVATE ERNEST WALKER
58160 2nd Battalion Welsh Regiment.
Died 23rd October 1918.

The 1911 Census shows Ernest's father, William, was employed as a telegraph wire man for the Great Central Railway. His family lived at 175 Thrumpton Lane..

Records show that Ernest, although born in Retford and living in Retford, enlisted in Derby.

It is highly likely that Ernest Walker was killed while the 2nd Battalion Welsh Regiment was involved in the Final Advance in Picardy. The 2nd Battalion Welsh Regiment were involved in the Battle of the Selle which took place between 17th and 25th October 1918.

Ernest Walker is buried in Highland Cemetery, Le Cateau, France.

PRIVATE HAROLD WILSON
29262 7th Battalion The Buffs (East Kent Regiment).
Died 26th October 1918.

Harold Wilson died of wounds, probably received in action during what became known as the Battle of the Selle. His records show that he was born in Hemsworth and was residing in Ordsall, Retford, at the time of his enlistment. According to the 1911 Census his parents lived at 81 Brecks Road.

Harold Wilson is buried at Quietiste Military Cemetery, Le Cateau, France.

SAPPER ALBERT HEWITT
140188 11th Field Company Royal Engineers.
Died 29th October 1918.

During the First World War, Le Treport was an important hospital centre and, by July 1916, the town contained three general hospitals: the 3rd, 16th and 2nd Canadian, No. 3 Convalescent Depot and Lady Murray's BRCS Hospital. The 7th Canadian, 47th and 16th USA General Hospitals arrived later, but all of the hospitals had closed by March 1919.

Sadly, it was at one of these hospitals that Sapper Albert Hewitt, aged thirty, died. Albert was the third son of Mr and Mrs Charles Hewitt, who lived at 26 Richard Street, Newtown. He died on 29th October 1918 of influenza and broncho-pneumonia.

Albert had joined the colours towards the end of 1915, crossing to France in the spring of 1916. Albert had been a scholar at the Council School and was a member of the

Congregational Sunday School. He had served his apprenticeship at Messrs Hurst and Son, builders, and was in their employ up to the time of enlisting. An elder brother, Ernest, was discharged from the Sherwood Foresters in July 1917, having seen a great deal of action and having been wounded three times at Epehy, Le Sars and Ypres.

Albert Hewitt was buried with full military honours in Mont Huon Cemetery, Le Treport, France.

PRIVATE FRANK BRIGGS
100215 25th Squadron Machine Gun Corps (Cavalry), formerly 4770 A/1st Sherwood Rangers Nottinghamshire Yeomanry.
Killed 30th October 1918.

Frank Briggs, son of George and Mary of 43 St John's Street, died in Mesopotamia on 30th October 1918. In 1911 he had a brother Joe and they were both employed as gardeners. Frank was twenty-eight years of age when he died.

Frank Briggs has no known grave and his name is commemorated on the Basra Memorial, Iraq.

SECOND LIEUTENANT ERNEST EAITCH
1st/17th (County of London)Battalion (Poplar and Stepney Rifles) London Regiment.
Died 2nd November 1918.

Ernest was born in 1897. His birthplace is shown as Eccleshall Bierlow, near Sheffield; his parents were Fred and Emily Eaitch. Fred died in 1898 and Emily married Charles Potter, a printer, and in 1911 the family was living at 68 Grove Street.

In 1916 Ernest married Nora Kedge and set up their marital home at Exton, 3 Danesbury Avenue, Southbourne, Bournemouth.

Ernest was wounded when the contents of an exploding gas shell affected both his lungs and he died before reaching the casualty clearing station.

Ernest Eaitch is buried in Laventie Military Cemetery, La Gorgue, France.

PRIVATE THOMAS ARTHUR BRADLEY
60757 30th Battalion Machine Gun Corps (Infantry).
Died 4th November 1918.

It was believed that Thomas Bradley died on 4th November 1918, possibly from wounds received. However, a later report, of 1919, suggested that he may have died as a prisoner of war on 30th October 1918, having been taken prisoner in March 1918. He was twenty-seven.

Thomas Bradley was the son of William and Louise Bradley, who lived at 39 Little Lane, Retford. At the time of his death his wife, Gertrude Florence, lived at 27 Moorgate with their only child. Before enlisting on 15th July 1916 he was employed at the Northern Rubber Works, having previously worked at Wharton and Long, Printers. He went to France in October 1916.

Thomas Bradley is buried in Terlincthun British Cemetery, Wimille, France.

PRIVATE JOSEPH EDWARD ROBINSON
41150 13th Battalion Royal Scots (Lothian Regiment), formerly 46318 Royal Scots Fusiliers.
Died 5th November 1918.

Joseph Robinson was the son of John and Jane Robinson, who lived at Station Street in Tuxford. He was born at Grasby in Lincolnshire. Sadly, Joseph died two days after his twenty-first birthday, as a prisoner of war. The news was first received in the Robinson household via letter from a soldier friend of Joseph who was in the same hospital.
Prior to enlisting, Joseph worked at Marshalls greengrocers, and the Retford Co-operative. He had joined up on 6th September 1916 and, following training at Chelmsford, went overseas. He had been wounded on two previous occasions.

Joseph was wounded in action on 28th March 1918, sustaining a fractured thigh due to bullet wounds. A fortnight before the letter announcing his death was received, his parents had received a letter from Joseph himself, telling them that all was well. He was buried with full military honours in the grounds of Wessel Hospital and was moved after the war.

John Robinson is buried in Cologne Southern Cemetery, Germany.

GUNNER HARRY TURNER
95914 Royal Garrison Artillery 244 Siege Battery
Died 6th November 1918.

Harry Turner was married to Alice and had a daughter, Dorothy. They lived in Thrumpton Lane. Before enlisting, Harry was employed by Messrs Laxenby and Milner, coal merchants, as a carter.

It was noted in the Retford Times that Harry once 'bravely gave' 1½ pints of blood 'to save a chum'. The Great War had seen huge advancements in blood transfusions, but the process was still in its infancy.

Harry died of wounds on 6th November 1918 in the 26th General Hospital at Etaples. He was thirty-four years of age. He had been admitted to the hospital the day before with serious chest and abdomen wounds.

Harry Turner is buried at Etaples Military Cemetery, France.

SERGEANT GEORGE DAVISON

13016 1st Battalion Yorkshire Regiment.
Killed on 6th November 1918.

Under the headline "Three Soldier Brothers: two killed, the third a prisoner", the death was announced of Sergeant George Davison of the 2nd Battalion Yorkshire Regiment; he had been killed in action by machine gun fire.

The headline alluded to the fact that George's older brother, Walter, had been killed on 28th August 1915 (see above) whilst serving with the 10th Battalion Sherwood Foresters and the eldest brother, Pte Arthur Davison, also a Sherwood Forester, was taken prisoner on 4th April 1917.

Having been taken prisoner, Arthur was employed on the land and railways near Stuttgart for a year.

He was released on 17th November 1918, finally reaching Retford on 8th December 1918 (He was granted two months' leave).

George, the son of Mrs Mary Denis Davison and the late Mr Arthur Davison, of 12 Hospital Road, served his apprenticeship with Messrs Jenkins and Company. He enlisted in the Regulars on 2nd September 1914 whilst employed by Messrs John Brown and Company of Sheffield. Having undergone training in Wendover and Tring, George embarked for France on 11th September 1915, a year and nine days after enlisting. He fought through the Battles of Loos and the Somme, acting for most of the time as stretcher-bearer to his company. He was last in Retford for Christmas 1917. His officer, Lieutenant Williams, wrote to his mother stating that "her son was one of their best sergeants and always did his duty cheerfully and conscientiously".
He was twenty-five years of age.

George Davison is buried at Bettrechies Communal Cemetery in France.

DRIVER WILLIAM WILLIAMSON

45528 "C" Battery, 94th Brigade, Royal Field Artillery.
Died 13th November 1918.

William Williamson was the son of Frederick and Emily Jane Williamson and was married to Eleanor Williamson of 82 Cobwell Road. He was just twenty-five years of age when he succumbed to influenza and died just two days after the Armistice.

The Brigade Diary tells us that on 23rd October 1918 'B' and 'C' Batteries moved forward into action south of Ovillers at about 11.00 hours, followed by 'D' and 'B' Batteries just before dusk. Eventually the Brigade HQ was established at Ovillers.

On 24th October 1918 "An attack at 04.00 hours on Poix du Nord by 62nd and 64th Infantry Brigades were supported by fire from all Batteries. This attack succeeded and 'A', 'B' and 'D' Batteries moved forward to a position east of Vendegies just in time to fire a barrage for an attack at 16.00 hours to capture ground of a tactical importance east of Poix du Nord. 'C' Battery, which had become much reduced in personnel owing to evacuation due to influenza, did not move forward from its position in Ovillers."

The actions mentioned above were all part of the Battle of the Selle, which took place between 17th and 25th October 1918.

William Williamson is buried in St Sever Cemetery Extension, Rouen, France.

Photograph of William Williamson's grave in St Sever Cemetery Extension in Rouen, (supplied by Sydney Barthorpe, a relative).

SAPPER DANIEL WOODWARD
WR/257927 Railway Operating Department, Royal Engineers.
Died 14th November 1918.

Daniel was born in 1891, the son of Charles, a boot sole maker at the Northern Rubber Works, and Charlotte Woodward. In 1911 the family was living at 13 Century Road and Daniel was employed as an engine cleaner at one of the local locomotive depots.

His next of kin is listed as his brother-in-law, Walter Thorpe, who lived at Ship Inn Cottage on Wharf Road.

Daniel Woodward is buried at Abbeville Communal Cemetery Extension, France.

PRIVATE FREDERICK WILLIAM DAVIES
46295 1st Battalion King's Own Yorkshire Light Infantry
Died 15th November 1918.

On 6th December 1918 news finally reached the home of Mr and Mrs Alfred Davies (Meech House, Ollerton Road) that their son Frederick (aged twenty) had succumbed to wounds received on 9th November 1918, probably fighting in the Battle of the Sambre. He had received wounds to both legs resulting in amputation and eventually the loss of his life.

The deceased had a brother, Alf, who served in the ASC and survived the war, and was the brother-in-law of Edward Howgate, who was killed in 1917 whilst serving with the Lincolns. Coincidentally both Frederick and Edward are buried in the same cemetery in Rouen. At the time of his death Frederick was engaged to Miss A. Elsom, who, with his parents, attended a memorial service following his death at All Hallows Church, Ordsall.

Frederick Davies is buried in St Sever Cemetery Extension, Rouen, France.

PRIVATE WALTER WILLIS
M/416924 M.T. Depot (Sydenham) Army Service Corps.
Died 24th November 1918

Walter was the son of Mr and Mrs Frank Willis of Glebe Farm, North Road, Retford. He had previously been employed by the Doncaster Corporation at their Electricity Works. Walter died in Croydon, probably of influenza.

Walter Willis is buried in the East Retford Baptist Chapelyard (now The Well).

STOKER 1ST CLASS JOHN (JACK) SUTTON
SS/112473 HMS P67, Royal Navy.
Died 27th November 1918.

Jack Sutton (born 10th June 1894), whose parents lived at 71 West Street, had taken part in the Battle of Jutland, and died on 27th November 1918 following seven months in Winter Street Hospital, Sheffield (now the School of Nursing and Midwifery, Sheffield). A report in the Retford Times states that Jack's nerves were "shattered." The Royal Navy and Royal Marine War Graves Roll gives the cause of death as "Died from disease". Jack had been in the Navy for six years.

At some stage Jack had volunteered for secret service and served on a Q Ship P67. "These were built under the Emergency War Programme. Designed as P-boats, these crafts were converted or modified while being built, to act as Submarine Decoy Vessels or "Q-boats". The four-inch gun was hidden behind various forms of dummy loads, e.g., bales or packing cases of merchandise or trusses of hay. In some boats it was located within a collapsible pantechnicon furniture van, or under a dummy boat built in folding sections. It was expected that, on account of shallow draught, torpedoes fired by U-boats would under-run these PC-boats, while, if hit by torpedo, bulge protection and special fillings would keep them afloat long enough to destroy the U-boat. (Jane's Fighting Ships 1919).

Jack's brother Harry was killed whilst serving with the 1st Battalion Sherwood Forests in 1917.

Jack Sutton is buried in East Retford Cemetery.

HMS P.67, a Q ship, which had two aliases: Chintz & Flashlight. Built by S.White in 1917 she survived the war.

SERGEANT PERCY WILLIAM DOE

MM 200248 1st/4th Battalion Lincolnshire Regiment transferred to (619586) Clearing Office Labour Corps.
Died 23 Jan 1919.

Percy William Doe was the son of George and Elizabeth. Percy was the eldest child having two sisters and a brother.

Under the headline "Another Distinction for Retford" the following report was printed announcing the award of the Military Medal to Percy William Doe.

"Sergeant Percy William Doe. 1/4th Lincolns, son of Mr G W Doe of Thrumpton Lane, Retford has been awarded the Military Medal for distinguished service. The official record of the gallant deed, which gained him his much-coveted distinction, is as follows: 'On the night of February 15th (1917) at Hannescamps the NCO was out on patrol under 2nd Lieutenant J R Neave*; two hostile patrols were encountered which had to be dealt with at the same time. Both hostile patrols were attacked and driven off in disorder, leaving one corpse behind. The success of our patrol was due to a great extent to the cool and clever handling of the Lewis Gun by Sgt Doe. He kept the firing as long as was needed, in spite of three stoppages occurring, which he skilfully rectified'.

Further Account from an extract form Major C.R.Simpson's History of the Lincolnshire Regiment 1914-1918

"An incident in no-man's-land whilst the 4th Battalion held the trenches in the Hannescamps sector has to be mentioned. A patrol of 'C' Company under 2nd Lt J.R. Neave, on the Hannescamps to Essarts road, about six hundred yards from their own lines, on the 15th February, was surrounded by strong enemy patrols. Fortunately, the Lincolnshires had a Lewis Gun under Sgt Doe, and, with great gallantry, the patrol fought its way against the Germans, and established itself in some old gun-pits, whence the enemy was beaten off and compelled to retire to his own lines. The patrol found the body of a dead German, and brought it back to the trenches. The 1/4th was congratulated by the General Officer Commanding the Division, and the Brigade Commander, 2nd Lt Neave was awarded the MC, and Sgt Doe and Cpl Fluke the MM."

"The gallant young soldier was educated at the National School and when he finished gained an apprenticeship at Messrs Robey's Engineering Works, Lincoln. He was only twenty years of age and was a member of the Lincoln Territorials. When war was declared he was on camp with his regiment at Bridlington. He went into training and was in and out of various camps and went out to France two years ago and has seen a lot of hard fighting. On one occasion many of his section were killed and wounded and on another occasion at Hill 60 he was buried and had a very narrow escape. But so far he has happily come through without serious injury. He was home on leave last April (1916), looking remarkably well. He was then a Lance Corporal and has since been made a Sergeant. In conveying the news of his success to his parents, the brave young soldier says that the General shook hands with him and congratulated him as the first with the Battalion to win the Military Medal in 'no-man's-land.'"

Percy survived the rest of the war, but on the 31st January 1919, under the headline "Retford Military Funeral", The Retford Times wrote:

"Deep sympathy is felt in Retford for Mr and Mrs Doe, Thrumpton, in the loss they have sustained by the death of their second son, Sergeant Percy W Doe MM 1 /4 Lincolns. He passed away last Thursday at the Winter Street Military Hospital, Sheffield. He had been a patient in France for five weeks, suffering from influenza and congestion of the lungs, and was removed to Sheffield on the last day of 1918. He went through the whole campaign up to the Armistice and this was the first time he had been in hospital. He was twenty-two years of age. A younger brother, Pte GE Doe, Sherwood Foresters, is in France. The internment took place at the Retford Cemetery and the deceased was accorded a military funeral. The firing party came from the RAF and Pte Briggs, Newtown (a part of Retford) sounded the Last Post.................."

Percy Doe is buried in East Retford Cemetery.

GUNNER JOSEPH VICTOR PIGGOTT
2232 2nd Australian Field Artillery Brigade, formerly 1st Battalion Light Horse Regiment, 15th Reinforcement, Australian Imperial Force.
Died 25th October 1919

Joseph Victor Piggott was the son of Francis and Sarah Piggott. The 1911 Census shows the family living at 46 Grove Lane, with Joseph employed as an apprentice engineer.

In 1913 Joseph Piggott moved to Cobbadah in New South Wales, Australia and began a new career as a school teacher. With the outbreak of war, Joseph enlisted, at nearby Armidale, on 10th November 1915. On 21st March 1916 he embarked from Sydney aboard HMAT Armadale A26.

The London Gazette dated 12th July 1918 announced that Joseph had been awarded the Belgian Croix de Guerre "for distinguished services rendered during the course of the campaign".

At the conclusion of the war, on 5th January 1919, Joseph returned to Australia, but during his time in France he had become ill with diabetes and he returned home to Retford, where he died of complications later that year.

The following individuals, who lost their lives in the First World War, are also commemorated on the memorial:

Frank Armstrong	Albert E Orr
Fred Barlow	William Hardy Palmer
Ernest William Bird	George H Parker
Arthur Clark	Thomas Pattison
Frederick Herbert Clarke	George Pawson
Bernard A Corke	William Peatfield
Charles Cowrie [Cowie]	John Redfern
F E V Davison	George C W Robinson
P E Davison	J Rutland
Harry Dexter	William A Seston
Harry Dixon	John Shaw
John P Dixon	Samuel Shaw
Richard Ford	Ernest Smith
Joseph Grande	George J Smith
Albert Harris	Harry Smith
George Hartley	James Smith
James Ernest Hindley	Nathaniel Smith
Herbert Hollingsworth	T Smith
Arthur C Houlden	C W Taylor
Fred Jackson	Thomas Taylor
David James	William Thompson
Cecil William Jarman	Thomas Tinker
J W Jowett	George Turner
Thomas Jubb	Andrew Ward
C W Lindley	Jack West
Charles Liversidge	Tom Wilkinson
Fred Harold Loftus	William Wilkinson
Edgar Markham	George Williams
John Markham	Herbert Winter
Robert Martin	A Wood
Sidney Milner	Tom Yoell
John Morley	

Panel 1

STANLEY ADWICK
WILLIAM ALLEN
JOHN WM ALLISON
JOHN ANDERSON
GEORGE BALDOCK
F. BANNISTER. SEN.
F. BANNISTER. JUN
FREDK WM BARBER
FRED BARLOW
WILLIAM BEARDSALL
DAVID BELL
WALTER BELL
WILLIE BELL
FRANK BENNETT
FRANK BETSON
H TOMLINSON BIRKETT
ERNEST WM BIRD
WALTER EDWARD BLAKE
W BOOTH
THOMAS ARTHUR BRADLEY
CHARLES BRAMMER
ERNEST BREDDY
JAMES BREDDY
JOHN BREDDY
WILLIAM BREDDY
FRANK BRIGGS
LEONARD BRIGGS
EDWARD BROUGHTON
SYDNEY BROUGHTON
A BROWN
NOEL BUTTON
EDWARD CASBURNE
CAMPBELL CAWOOD
CHARLES M. CHAPMAN
JOHN CHAPMAN
ARTHUR C. CHANDLER
L. CHANDLER
JOHN COOLING

Panel 2

ARTHUR CLARK
FREDK HBT CLARKE
REGINALD W. CLARK
P. CLEMENTS
W. H. COLLINGBURN
SAMUEL COOK
WILFRID COOKE
GEORGE COOKE
HERBERT COOLING
G. W. COOPER
JAMES CORDALL
BERNARD A. CORKE
THOMAS H. COWLING
CHARLES COWRIE
GEORGE COX
HERBERT CRISP
HERBERT CROSSLAND
J. C. CUTLER
J. W. DARWIN
F. W. DAVIES
F. E. V. DAVISON
G. DAVISON
HORACE DAVISON
L. B. DAVISON
WALTER DAVISON
P. E. DAVISON
WILLIAM DAWSON
HARRY DEXTER
HARRY DIXON
JOHN ARTHUR DIXON
JOHN P. DIXON
LESLIE DIXON
JOHN DODSON
P. W. DOE
ROBERT J. DRAKEFIELD
GEORGE H. DUDDRIDGE
JOSEPH DIXON
RICHARD FORD

Panel 3

JOHN DUGDALE
ERNEST EAITCH
JOHN RADLEY EDDISON
FRED EDE
ARTHUR ENDERBY
WILLIAM EYRE
FRANK FARRAND
FRANK J. FLINTON
A. FRARY
WALTER FUGUEL
ARTHUR FULLARD
ROBERT COLTON GAGG
GEORGE WM GAUTREY
GEORGE GILL
WILLIAM GLEADEN
CHARLES GRANDE
JOSEPH GRANDE
CHARLES H. GRANT
H. GRANT
ALBERT HARRIS
F. HARRISON
G. C. HARRISON
GEOFFREY C. HARRYMAN
GEORGE HARTLEY
HARRY HASLAM
GEO. WM HAUGHTON
ABRAHAM HEATH
EDGAR HEEDS
ALFRED HEMPSALL
JOHN HEMPSHALL
ALBERT HEWITT
A. E. HEWITT
HORACE E. HIGGS
J. D. HILTON
ALBERT E. HINCKS
JAMES ERNEST HINDLLY
EDGAR HIRST
ALFRED HEWITT

Panel 4

JOHN EDGAR HURST HIRST
ED LINTON HODSON
J. W. HODSON
WALTER HOLEY
WILLIAM HOLLAND
C. W. HOLLIDAY
TREVOR HOLLIDAY
HBT HOLLINGSWORTH
ARTHUR C. HOULDEN
ALFRED T. HOWGATE
ED ARTHUR HOWGATE
ALFRED HOWLETT
B. C. HUNTSMAN
HERBERT HUSBAND
GEO. WILLIAM INGALL
SIDNEY JACKSON
FRED JACKSON
DAVID JAMES
CECIL WM JARMAN
JOSEPH JOHNSON
JAMES WM JOHNSON
J. W. JOWETT
THOMAS JUBB
HERBERT KAYE
E. KING
CHARLES H. KIRTON
J. W. LACEY
JOE LAMB
V. C. LAND
ALLEN LEE
WILLIAM HAROLD LEE
CHARLES LEVICK
C. W. LINDLEY
SIDNEY LISTER
T. N. LISTER
CHARLES LIVERSIDGE
FRANK ARMSTRONG
L/CPL. MELLIGAN C.MP. 39/45

GEO. LIVERSIDGE
FRED HAROLD LOFTUS
EDGAR MARKHAM
JOHN MARKHAM
WILLIAM HILEY MARKHAM
EDWARD MARSH
JOHN MARSH
THOMAS HENRY MARSH
ROBERT MARTIN
WILLIAM MEAD
G. MERRILLS
WILLIAM MERRILLS
C. WALTER MERRYWEATHER
SIDNEY MILLER
CHARLES MILLINGTON
SIDNEY MILNER
F. MORLEY
JOHN MORLEY
G.E MORRIS
F.S. MORTON
HAROLD MOTTASHED
JABEZ MOUNTAIN
JAMES Ed NEWSTEAD
ALFRED NICHOLSON
ARTHUR MARSHALL OAKDEN
ALBAN OFFORD
ALBERT E. ORR
CHARLES OSTICK
FRED OSTICK
GEORGE OSTICK
HARRY WRIGHT OSTICK
HORACE PALETHORPE
JIM PALETHORPE
WM HARDY PALMER
JACK PARKIN
GEORGE H. PARKER
ALFRED PATTISON
WILLIAM HOULT 39/45

THOS. PATTISON
WALTER PATTISON
WILLIAM PATTISON
VINCENT PATTISON
GEORGE PAWSON
WM PEATFIELD
JOHN PERRON
JAMES PETTINGER
A. PHILLIPSON
FRANK PICKARD
JOSEPH V. PIGGOTT
ROBERT SYDNEY PLANT
HARRY RANDALL
WALTER RANDALL
HERBERT RAYNOR
JOHN REDFERN
ALFRED REGISTER
W.N. REYNOLDS
WM RICHARDSON
GEO. C.W. ROBINSON
JOHN ROBINSON
J.H. ROBINSON
J. EDWARD ROBINSON
WALTER C. ROGAN
VALENTINE W. ROGERS
JOHN ROSSINGTON
RICHARD ROSSINGTON
J. RUTLAND
ARTHUR SANDERSON
SAM SANDERSON
HERBERT SAUNDERS
PERCY SCOTT
WILLIAM A. SESTON
JOHN SHAW
J. HERBERT SHAW
SAMUEL SHAW
HARRY SMITH
NATHANIEL SMITH

ARTHUR SLINGSBY
ROBERT SLY
ALBERT E. SMITH
ERNEST SMITH
GEORGE J. SMITH
JAMES SMITH
T. SMITH
THOMAS J. SMITH
FRANK SNOWDEN
ALFRED SPENCER
J.W. SPENCER
GEORGE SPRAY
JAMES SPRAY
MARK STANLEY
FRANK STOCKDALE
F.J. STOCKDALE
WALTER STOCKDALE
CHARLES STOCKS
HARRY SUMMERSCALES
ALBERT SUTTON
H. SUTTON
JACK SUTTON
HENRY SWANNACK
CYRIL SWIFT
CHARLES TALBOT
H. TALBOT
G.W. TALLENTS
DAVID TANNER
C.W. TAYLOR
EDWIN H. TAYLOR
GEORGE GILBERT TAYLOR
THOS. TAYLOR
WILLIAM TAYLOR
JOHN T THOMPSON
WM THOMPSON
J.W. THEAKER
G.W. TINKER
GEORGE TURNER

THOMAS TINKER
G. TOMLINSON
JAMES TOMLINSON
LEONARD TOMLINSON
B.W. TOWNROW
HARRY TURNER
J. TURNER
H. VALLANCE
S VALLANCE
HAROLD M VESSEY
WILLIAM WADE
W.H. WALKER
ERNEST WALKER
ANDREW WARD
SAMUEL WARDLE
HAROLD WATERFIELD
ALFRED WELTON
JACK WEST
EDGAR C. WHITE
GEORGE WHITLAM
COLIN WILLIAMS
GEORGE WILLIAMS
WILLIAM WILLIAMSON
HAROLD WILLIS
WALTER WILLIS
TOM WILKINSON
HERBERT WINTER
REGINALD P. WINTOUR
A. WOOD
REGINALD H WOOD
CHARLES WOODWARD
DANIEL WOODWARD
JOHN WOODWARD
B.S. WOOLNER
ERNEST WORTHINGTON
TOM YOELL
WILLIAM WILKINSON
HAROLD WILSON

LOCAL NEWSPAPERS FOLLOWED THE PROGRESS OF THE FUND-RAISERS

APPEAL BOOST: Bassetlaw Council chairman Coun Wendy Quigley hands over a cheque for £5,000 to the memorial restoration committee

Cash boost for memorial fund

THE campaign to raise money to refurbish Retford's war memorial has received a boost following a donation by Bassetlaw Council.

The council presented the Retford War Memorial Restoration Fund with £5,000 this week.

The donation brings the total raised to around £15,000.

Those behind the restoration hope to refurbish fully the memorial to bring it back to its former glory.

Around £20,000 is needed to restore the memorial which stands in the market square.

The funding raised so far includes a pledge of £2,500 from the Percy Law Fund and £2,000 from the Retford Civic Society for a display board outlining the history of the memorial and other information.

Project co-ordinator Ken Hoddy said: "We are grateful the council has donated this money which will help us take a step closer towards starting the restoration work."

Council leader Mike Quigley said they are working closely with the committee to help get the memorial restored.

"It has always been this council's position that if the application for funding was unsuccessful we would make up the shortfall.

"We hope work will start on the memorial in June following talks with the chosen contractors."

The committee is also currently awaiting a decision by Notts County Council on funding from the BBC fund.

Memorial fund reaches target

MONTHS of fund-raising mean Retford's War Memorial will now be restored to its former glory.

The restoration fund has been supported by local councils, organisations, businesses and members of the public to reach the target of £20,000.

Following talks with Retford Town Centre Manager Russell Slater, a contractor has now been chosen -Retford Memorials - and a schedule of work drawn up to begin in June.

They will look after the entire project - rebuffing bronze plates, replacing missing chains and pavings, and re-cutting weathered names.

The work will take about a month, after which an unveiling and re-dedication of the memorial will take place in August.

The campaign received a

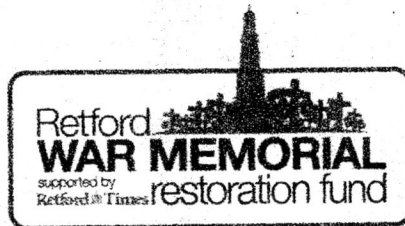

Retford **WAR MEMORIAL** supported by Retford Times restoration fund

massive fund-raising boost following a donation by Bassetlaw Council, which presented the Retford War Memorial Restoration Fund with £5,000.

They needed £20,000 to restore the memorial, which stands in the market square.

Pledges from The Percy Law Fund, Retford Civic Society, Retford District Council, Unison Worksop Branch and Notts County Council's Building Better Communities Initiative (BBC) among others, have helped secure this amount.

Charities, businesses and individuals all did their bit.

The *Retford Times* has sup-

ported the campaign from the start with publicity and flyers, raising awareness and rallying supporters.

But it was the motivation and perseverance of a group of ex-servicemen that kept the project's momentum going to reach its successful conclusion.

Project coordinator Ken Hoddy said it was a fantastic outcome, and thanked all who have supported it.

"The memorial cost only £1,800 to create originally yet it's costing £20,000 to restore - it was a lot of money to raise so it is great news we have achieved our target and secured a contractor for work to commence.

"Raising the funds has been a collaborative effort, with generous donations from those who care about our town. A big 'well done' goes to Retford!"

Rededication Ceremony 2008

After the restoration work had been completed, the memorial was rededicated on Sunday 17th August 2008. At 10.30am over 600 people gathered to witness the event and the Whitwell Brass Band played the Olympic Fanfare to start the ceremony.

The Master of Ceremonies, Graham Bonnyman, welcomed dignitaries, representatives of Associations and member of the public to the ceremony. Local military historian, Tom Champion, was among those to address the public. Mr Champion, who was the first to put forward the idea of refurbishing the memorial, spoke of its history. He was followed by another local historian, Tim Bethell, who spoke about some of the named soldiers on the memorial. Father Bill Bergin led the prayer and then gave a sermon. The formal rededication was made by Patrick Mercer, Retford's MP, who finished with the following words:

For those who died in war and conflict,
For all those who have been missed and mourned them,
For all scarred by war and conflict,
Land impoverished and people driven to despair,
Grant them light, hope and peace.
Let us pray for Elizabeth our Queen,
For all set in authority under her and for leaders of the nations:
Grant them cool heads, firm hands, warm hearts and ears open to God's will.

WE WILL REMEMBER THEM

The Rededication ceremony

Patrick Mercer O.B.E. M.P. Rededicated the Memorial 17th August 2008

Frank Price M.B.E. Chairman of the Retford War Memorial Restoration Committee

MEMORIAL PLANTER: Father Bill Bergin dedicates the planter for crosses at the memorial in the Market Square.

Addition to war memorial

A NEW cross planter has been placed on the North side of the Retford War Memorial to accommodate an overflow of crosses planted this year.

The new planter has been sponsored by ex-servicemen from The Fellowship of the Services 273 Retford Cannon Mess. The first cross planter was so full members of the public had to be placed in turf with no protection from weather damage. This second planter will now accommodate all the crosses.

Organiser Ken Hoddy said: "Now we have had a wonderful restoration of our memorial and the two planters, next month when the new floodlights are switched on it should look spectacular.

"A worthy tribute to the 416 names it commemorates."

March 2011

PRESENTED BY
LOCAL EX-SERVICEMEN
OF THE 273.
RETFORD CANNON MESS.
THE FELLOWSHIP
OF THE SERVICES.
MARCH 2011.

WE WILL REMEMBER THEM

The Battlefield Cross

On Sunday 17th August a ceremony was held at the memorial by Retford Veterans (ex-servicemen) to bless a memorial cross for all those soldiers who died in the First World War, but have no known grave; the blessing was given by Father Bill Bergin.

The Battlefield Cross signifies the tumultuous events that began exactly 100 years ago. The cross is made of oak and carries the inscription 'Known Unto God'. The hat attached to the top of the cross is a genuine first issue helmet of WWI which was recovered from a battlefield in the Somme region, and the damage to the top of it clearly shows damage from action on the battlefield. The cross was made by a retired Retford joiner, and represents the temporary wooden crosses used during WWI as battlefield grave-markers.

This small but significant memorial serves to remind us of the great sacrifice made by 306 Retford heroes during the Great War, many of whom have no known grave, but are 'Known Unto God'.

Retford veterans and Father Bill Bergin at the blessing of the Battlefield Cross.

*Crowds gather around the War Memorial 100 years after the start
of the First World War.*